Diesels on the Western

MICHAEL WELCH

Capital Transport

ISBN 978-1-85414-367-9

Published by
Capital Transport Publishing Ltd
www.capitaltransport.com

Printed by Parksons Graphics

Front cover: The old days at Williton. Today Williton station is a crossing point on the highly successful preserved West Somerset Railway and the locomotive works that has been developed on the left of the picture beyond the goods shed is a constant hive of activity. When this shot was taken of a 'Hymek' pulling out with the 10.25am Minehead to Paddington on 13th June 1970 the outlook for the Minehead to Taunton line was bleak indeed and passenger services were withdrawn from the line in January 1971, six months after this scene was recorded. A six-car DMU rake, *en route* to Minehead, waits patiently in the down loop. *John Spencer Gilks*

Title Page: 'But we always mend the track on Sundays'. A small army of permanent way men stands to one side as a 'Western' gingerly approaches with (what is believed to be) the up 'Cornish Riviera Express', passing 'Warship' No.D812 *Royal Naval Reserve 1859-1959* on the civil engineer's departmental duties. Note the total lack of high visibility clothing in this picture which was taken at the site of the former Somerton station on 21st March 1965. *Mike Jose*

Back cover top: A distinguished and colourful visitor. 'Western' C-C No.D1015 *Western Champion,* in golden ochre livery, is seen at Wolverhampton (Low Level) in March 1963. The headcode indicates that it may have just been uncoupled from the 1.10pm Paddington-Birmingham (Snow Hill)-Birkenhead (Woodside) express. *Russell Leitch/Colour Rail.com*

Back cover bottom: Built on the site of a former Bristol & Exeter Railway locomotive shed, Bristol Bath Road depot was closed to steam traction in September 1960 and reopened as a diesel depot in late 1961. In this picture taken on 1st November 1969 'Westerns' and 'Hymeks' can be seen rubbing shoulders with an assortment of other types. Bath Road depot was closed in September 1995. *Hugh Ballantyne*

Introduction

If you mention the names *Greyhound* or *Western Ranger* to the average diesel enthusiast his eyes will immediately light up because they represent two of the best-loved classes from the early BR diesel era. The 'Western' always did things differently and probably did not surprise anybody when it opted for hydraulic rather electric transmission for its diesel locomotives. The result was one of the most distinctive fleets that really gave the Western Region (WR) a special identity which was enhanced by Swindon-built diesel units that had their own special characteristics. This album looks back at the WR scene as it was during the first two decades or so of diesel operation.

The forerunner of the Western Region was, of course, the Great Western Railway (GWR) who experimented with diesel traction way back in the 1930s. A 121hp vehicle, a joint venture between the Associated Equipment Company and Park Royal Coachworks Ltd, began operation from Reading in December 1933 and the car proved so successful a further three were ordered for express services. Regular operation started on the Birmingham to South Wales route in 1934. The GWR also took an interest in developments with diesel locomotive traction and in April 1936 took delivery of No.2, a 350hp shunter built by Hawthorn Leslie that was similar to those entering service with the LMSR but further developments were halted by the outbreak of war in 1939.

In the early 1950s some diesel shunters entered traffic but it was 1955 before BR announced its Modernisation Plan, heralding the end of steam traction which would be replaced by diesel and electric motive power. The Western Region hierarchy had been impressed by developments in Germany, where high-speed diesel hydraulic locomotives were making their mark, and decided to 'go it alone' and, amazingly, the British Transport Commission (BTC) gave its blessing to hydraulic transmission for the WR's main line diesel fleet when the other regions were opting for electric transmission. This was at a time when BR was still building 'standard' steam locomotives for general use!

The next major milestone was the entry into regular traffic of the North British (NBL) A1A-A1A Type 4 locomotives in June 1958. The NBL Type 4s were heavy and not quite what the WR wanted but shortly after they made their debut the first of the Swindon-built B-B 'Warships' took to the rails. These lightweight machines, modelled on the German 'V200' locomotives, were scaled down to fit the British loading gauge and, most importantly, incorporated Maybach engines with hydraulic transmission and met the WR's requirements admirably. Construction of these machines was split between Swindon and NBL, but those built by NBL were fitted with MAN engines that were prone to oil leaks and other defects which resulted in reduced reliability. The first locomotives of an order for NBL Type 2 locomotives, essentially equivalent to half of one of the same manufacturer's A1A-A1A Type 4s, appeared in January 1959 but these machines were not a resounding success, probably due to the failure of NBL, a renowned builder of steam engines, to adapt to diesel traction.

The first BR/Sulzer 1Co-Co1 Type 4 'Peaks' began crew training at Bristol in the spring of 1961 and these locomotives were destined to dominate services on the North East/South West route until ousted by HSTs in the early 1980s. May 1961 also saw No.D7000 enter traffic; this was the doyen of the Beyer Peacock Type 3 1,700hp B-B 'Hymeks', a class that arguably proved to be the most successful of the hydraulic designs. These machines were mainly used on semi-fast passenger and fitted freight workings, a total of 101 eventually being built in three separate batches. The 'Hymeks' were particularly associated with the Paddington to Worcester/Hereford services which they dominated for almost eight years. The year 1961 proved to be the most significant in the history of diesel development on the WR because in December the first of the 2,700hp 'Western' Class C-C locomotives, No.D1000 *Western Enterprise* emerged from Swindon works. The design was elegant and stylish and its experimental 'desert sand' livery ensured that the 'Western' Class made an immediate impact on railway aficionados and maybe even some members of the general public. Later sister engines were out-shopped in maroon, and green, while No.D1015 *Western Champion* was painted in 'golden ochre', so the variety of liveries added a real splash of colour to the scene. The WR organised a questionnaire to seek the views of young enthusiasts but this was regarded with some scepticism because the final decision to adopt maroon was reportedly taken by the region's General Manager, so the poll was a charade! The class took over the Paddington-Wolverhampton trains completely in September 1962 but many were soon out of action, largely due to transmission failures. Towards the end of their careers, however, they proved a huge asset due to the unreliability of other types and remained at work long past their intended withdrawal date thanks to the ability of the staff at Laira who cannibalised condemned locomotives to keep the remaining fleet operational. Laira also repainted locomotives to restore some dignity to machines with bodywork in poor condition.

Late 1963 saw the arrival of one of the ubiquitous Brush Type 4s on the WR, a class that later became a familiar sight on most parts of the Region. In mid-1964 No.D9500, a Type 1 650hp 0-6-0 locomotive designed for yard shunting and trip working, emerged from Swindon, the first of a class that was very much a 'white elephant', because that type of work was already declining and almost all of the locomotives were sold to outside industry after just a few years in traffic on BR.

The WR also had its own ideas when it came to DMUs, and in 1956 Swindon works had produced the first of a series of 'Inter City' units for use on the Birmingham to Cardiff service but these were quickly displaced by Swindon-built 'Cross Country' sets. Both fleets had only two cab windows unlike most DMU fleets that had three, while the 'Cross Country' units were also fitted with GWR-style suspended gangways so, predictably, these Swindon products were quite distinctive. A separate series of 'Cross Country' units was also produced by the Gloucester Railway Carriage & Wagon Co. for use on the WR. The later batch of 'Inter-City' units, which appeared in 1963 were, at least in the author's opinion, one of the finest first generation DMUs produced. They were equipped with B4 bogies, good sound insulation, distinctive driver's wrap-round windows and exceptionally comfortable seating in both saloons and compartments; some units had a buffet car. This stock was fitted with end gangways providing access throughout an eight-car train; this enabled passengers travelling in a non-buffet set to obtain refreshments.

In the mid-1960s BR was losing traffic at an alarming rate and a National Traction Plan was formulated which earmarked non-standard types that were surplus to requirements for early elimination. Many of the unsuccessful NBL-built locomotives were withdrawn *en masse* on 3rd October 1971 and at the end of that month a total of thirty-two 'Warships' and Type 2 B-Bs – some of the latter still in green livery – could be seen congregated near St Philips Marsh depot, Bristol. The end came quietly for the last Swindon-built 'Warship' just over a year later when No.821 *Greyhound* worked a Bristol to Plymouth parcels train. The bulk of the 'Hymeks' were withdrawn in 1971/72, but the speed of withdrawals slackened and four examples survived until March 1975. By this time the WR had the entire fleet of the later English Electric Type 4s, and many Brush Type 4s, but these were a mixed blessing and despite being reduced in theory to a handful of turns on west-of-England trains 'Westerns' frequently deputised for failed locomotives, sometimes powering air-conditioned stock from which they were officially barred. The 'Warships' had simply faded away almost unnoticed but the 'Westerns' departure from the scene was marked by a host of rail tours, some of which had to be duplicated to meet demand, the type having become one of the most popular diesel classes on BR. The last four examples, Nos.1010/13/23/48, were taken out of traffic on 27th February 1977 and with them the short-lived hydraulic era on BR came to an end.

Compilation of this album has benefited from assistance given by Bob Dalton, Chris Evans, Dave Fakes, John Langford and Terry Phillips who have kindly read through the proof and suggested many corrections and improvements to the text that have greatly enhanced the final product and thanks are offered to these gentlemen. Bryan Gibson kindly assisted with the identification of some of the trains, while slides from the R.C. Riley collection were provided by Rodney Lissenden. Bob Dalton, who was employed in the WR Shopping Control, supplied historical information about the rolling stock fleets. Design and typesetting by Lucy Frontani and Cat Bond.

Michael Welch
Burgess Hill, West Sussex
December 2012

Contents

An old timer and a real oddity. Formerly Great Western Railway No.2, this locomotive is the oldest featured in this album, being built as long ago as 1936. It was constructed by Hawthorn Leslie and was the GWR's version of a diesel shunter design that had been supplied by that company to the LMSR. The locomotive weighed 51tons 10cwt and was fitted with an English Electric 350hp engine which powered two nose-suspended traction motors. It officially entered service in April 1936 and was re-numbered 15100 in March 1948; during its long career it was usually shedded at Swindon but also had stints at St Philip's Marsh, Bristol, and Southall. Withdrawn in April 1965, No.15100 was unceremoniously cut-up at George Cohen's, Morriston, yard in January 1966 and, perhaps, it could be said that such a historically significant machine deserved a better fate. It was photographed at Swindon on 10th March 1963; note the prominent works plate on the cabside which doubtless revealed that No.15100 was Hawthorn Leslie works No.3853. *Roy Denison*

FORMER GREAT WESTERN RAILWAY DIESEL SHUNTER

The last days of the delightful Bewdley to Woofferton branch. The platform at Newnham Bridge station is still wet after a shower of rain but the clouds have parted sufficiently to enable former GWR railcar No.W26W to be photographed in glorious early spring sunshine on 18th March 1961. The railcar was forming the 12.10pm Woofferton to Kidderminster train. The Woofferton to Tenbury Wells section was opened by the Shrewsbury & Hereford Railway on 1st August 1861 while the stretch onward to Bewdley was promoted by the Tenbury & Bewdley Railway and came into use on 13th August 1864. The section west of Tenbury Wells was closed completely by BR from 31st July 1961, the final trains running on 29th July. The government had also sanctioned the closure of the Tenbury Wells to Bewdley section but BR agreed to run one morning and one afternoon train between Tenbury Wells and Kidderminster, principally for the benefit of schoolchildren, on condition that they would be withdrawn after twelve months if patronage did not justify their retention. After exactly one year these services also ceased, the last trains running on Tuesday 31st July 1962 – a most unusual case of a passenger service being withdrawn in the middle of the week. *John Langford*

Former GWR railcar No.W22W pauses at Cleobury Mortimer forming the 3.05pm Saturdays only train from Tenbury Wells to Kidderminster, also on 18th March 1961. This car is one of a number of GWR railcars to have survived into preservation. Despite this shot having being taken thirteen years after nationalisation of the railways, this station with its distinctive pagoda waiting shelter (partially visible on the left) and conical-shaped water tower still exuded pure Great Western Railway atmosphere. Note the grounded horsebox on the right – one wonders what it was used for. Cleobury Mortimer was the starting point of a light railway whose platform was adjacent to the premises seen here; the line opened for passenger traffic on 20th November 1908. It was closed to passenger trains in 1938 and the Admiralty, which had an armaments depot at Ditton Priors, assumed control in 1957. The line finally closed completely in 1965. *Roy Patterson*

A further view of railcar No.W26W at Newnham Bridge on the same day, looking westwards. This particular car entered service in September 1940 and survived to become one of the last GWR railcars in traffic, being withdrawn in October 1962; it was eventually broken-up in August 1964. This 210hp vehicle weighed 35tons 13cwt and had seating accommodation for 48 persons. The train service along this scenic byway could hardly be described as lavish, a total of five services being advertised on weekdays only in each direction in the summer 1961 timetable. *John Langford*

Not all former GWR railcars were painted in BR green livery and here is No.W19W, resplendent in carmine and cream colours, waiting in the platform at Ledbury station before leaving with the 1.30pm Saturdays only train to Gloucester on 27th June 1959, just a couple of weeks or so before the service was withdrawn. No.W19W was exactly the same type of car as the two vehicles depicted in the previous three pictures, but it was unfortunate enough to be the first of this type to be withdrawn, an event which occurred in February 1960. In the mid-1940s this vehicle was loaned to the LNER for trials in the York area. *John Langford*

A delightful rural scene at Bromyard station showing former GWR railcars Nos.W33W and W38W forming a train to Worcester on 14th April 1962. It may not be apparent from the picture but these cars comprised a twin-coach unit and each vehicle had a driving cab at one end only. Car No.W33W was built at Swindon in 1941 while No.W38W appeared in 1942. The latter vehicle was originally paired with W37W but this was destroyed by fire on the Cheddar Valley line in 1947 and W38W ran for a time with W22W. In 1954, however, W33W, which was originally built as a double-ended car, was rebuilt with a corridor connection to run as a permanent replacement for W37W. When BR-built DMUs started to appear on the WR the decision was taken in 1960 to base all of the remaining vehicles at Southall and Worcester, but in the spring of 1961 all serviceable cars were concentrated at Worcester for use on the Bromyard, Tenbury Wells and Severn Valley lines which became the last haunts of these distinctive vehicles. W33W and W38W survived until August 1962 and the very last GWR railcars in BR service were withdrawn two months later. Bromyard was originally an intermediate station on the Worcester (Leominster Jct.) to Leominster line but the passenger service beyond Bromyard was an early casualty, being withdrawn from 15th September 1952, while the very last ordinary passenger trains ran to Bromyard on 5th September 1964. *Roy Denison*

They may have been members of one of the most numerous classes on BR but few people seem to have been sufficiently motivated to photograph the ubiquitous BR 350hp diesel shunters; after all they were not often seen thundering through Sonning cutting or hauling heavy goods trains over the summit at Dainton! In this typical scene from the 1970s – note the 'B.R.U.T.E.' trolley on the left and coaches on the right in blue and grey livery – No.08 591 is gainfully employed as station pilot at Carmarthen on 9th August 1975. At that time such duties were still commonplace throughout the railway system due to the large number of loco-hauled trains that needed a turnover engine, multi-portioned trains and the vast network of van trains that still abounded. Many large stations had more than one pilot engine and they were kept fully employed shunting to and fro within station limits on a multiplicity of tasks – how so much more interesting railways were even at that time. No.08 591 was one of the Crewe-built machines, and it is recorded that it was out-shopped in October 1959 as No.D3758 and its initial allocation was at Danygraig, Swansea. *Roy Denison*

Plymouth station lies on the fringe of the city centre and has a distinctive backdrop of inner-city Victorian terraced houses on the northern side of the station complex. The chimney-pots of Plymouth provide the background to this shot of No.08 954 shunting vans at the eastern end of the station on 20th March 1979. This is a sight hardly ever seen on today's rather characterless railway network following the loss of newspaper and parcels traffic to the roads. The first of these shunters entered traffic in October 1952 and by an incredible stroke of good fortune, bearing in mind this was a very numerous class, the photographer recorded No.08 954, one of the final batch of three which entered service in January 1963; it was originally No.D4184 and built at Darlington. *Roy Denison*

There have been some very strange rolling stock designs over the years and, at least in the author's opinion, one of the most unusual DMU types was the original Swindon 'Inter-City' units which were constructed primarily for use on the Birmingham to South Wales route and between Glasgow and Edinburgh. These three-car units, which were introduced in September 1956, were the first DMUs to be built on the long 63ft 5in underframe. They were obviously designed to provide as much operational flexibility as possible and were unique in having one driving motor coach with a standard full-width driving cab similar to the Swindon 'Cross Country' units while the other motor coach had a through corridor connection with a tiny 'half-width' driving cab similar to those on many Southern Region EMUs. This arrangement enabled two three-car sets to be coupled together with a corridor throughout the whole formation, though it is likely that vehicles with a 'half width' driving cab were sometimes formed intermediately within a unit during times of rolling stock shortages. In this picture a six-car rake of these units is depicted passing through Widney Manor station with a train from Birmingham to Carmarthen in 1959. Note the 'speed whiskers' and lining that have been applied to the corridor shield, and also the letter headcode. *Michael Mensing*

A further view of one of these unorthodox and most interesting units, this time showing a three-car formation near Acocks Green in 1959. The units consisted of two motor coaches, each seating 52 second class passengers, and a seven compartment trailer first with 42 seats, so there was a high proportion of accommodation for first class passengers. It should be noted, however, that in some units a small buffet area was provided in the latter vehicle and in these coaches the seating was reduced to 18 first class, with a further 12 unclassed seats in the buffet. The unit shown here appears to include a trailer first without a buffet. The carriage nearest to the camera is DMBSL No.W79089 which was built at Swindon and released to traffic in November 1956. This coach operated on the WR for almost three years, being transferred to the Scottish Region in October 1959, and all of its sister vehicles were also moved northwards at about the same time. W79089 is thought to have been based at Leith Central depot and worked on the Glasgow to Edinburgh route until it was made redundant by the introduction of Mk.2 stock worked by Class 27s on this service in May 1971. Some carriages survived for a little longer, being transferred to the Glasgow to Ayr/Stranraer line. Amazing though it may seem, these vehicles caught the eye of the managers of the Lamco iron-ore railway in Buchanan, Liberia, and five were overhauled at Glasgow works prior to being shipped abroad. *Michael Mensing*

ORIGINAL SWINDON-BUILT 'INTER-CITY' UNITS (CLASS 126)

Suburban services on the WR's routes in the Birmingham area were a stronghold of a large fleet of Derby-built three-car units that first appeared in April 1957. These 600hp units consisted of a driving motor brake second, trailer composite and driving motor second and could accommodate 28 first and 234 second class passengers. The units employed on the lines in the West Midlands were maintained at Tyseley depot but it should be noted that a large batch was based at Cardiff Cathays for service on the Welsh valley lines. These units, which had no toilet facilities, were notoriously uncomfortable with cramped seating and draughty doors and windows. One of the routes they worked was that between Birmingham and Stratford-upon-Avon and in this view one of these units is seen leaving Hall Green station with the 8.15am from Stratford-upon-Avon on 16th August 1959. Note the large goods yard in the background with its string of coal wagons and piles of coal for local domestic use – how times have changed! *Michael Mensing*

A steam age diesel train or a diesel age steam train? When BR's modernisation plan was unveiled in 1955 it heralded the end of steam traction but in reality the replacement of steam had already begun because the very first DMUs, apart from one or two oddities, actually appeared in the spring of 1954. They were Derby Lightweight units based in West Yorkshire. The Derby-built three-car suburban sets of the type seen here at Kingham on 19th May 1962 were introduced in 1957 so came onto the scene rather later; note that this unit is unlined. The identity of the train is unrecorded but it was probably the 3.45pm Evesham to Oxford service; doubtless passengers were impressed by the speed and, hopefully, cleanliness of the relatively new form of traction. At this time Kingham station still retained an infrequent steam service to Chipping Norton – the branch train is depicted on the left in this picture – and a service to Cheltenham which was withdrawn from 15th October 1962. *Colour Rail.com*

Above: Photographed against a barren and inhospitable mountainside, a quite smart looking Derby-built three-car suburban unit waits to leave Maerdy with a train to Porth on an unknown date in the early 1960s; the picture must have been taken prior to 15th June 1964 because the service was withdrawn from that date. These units were built in three batches, the first of which had four lamps on the cab front. The vehicle nearest to the camera is a driving motor brake second with a two-character headcode box and two lamps which indicate that it was from one of the later series. These units will always be associated with the South Wales valleys, being first introduced on 2nd December 1957 on routes north of Newport and their sphere of activity was enlarged a month later when they took over some workings in the Cardiff valleys from steam traction. In 1875 a large colliery opened at Maerdy, which is 900 feet above sea level, and this was followed fourteen years later by the introduction of passenger services to Porth, a junction on the Treherbert to Cardiff line. The huge mine survived to become the last productive colliery in the Rhondda, closing in 1986. Note the long lines of coal wagons just visible in this shot above the signal box, bearing testament to the massive output from this mine.
Colour Rail.com

It is often said that the management think they take all of the decisions but in reality it is the shunter who runs the railway, and when he is short of rolling stock to make up the scheduled train formations the livery of each vehicle is immaterial so long as the passengers have a train provided. Here, on a bright and sunny 5th August 1967, the 3.30pm Birmingham Snow Hill to Wolverhampton Low Level train, formed of a Derby-built three-car suburban unit, is seen between West Bromwich and Swan Village with a blue-liveried driving motor second leading the other two vehicles, both of which are still in traditional green livery. Judging by the almost spotless white dome above the cab the front carriage appears to be making one of its first sorties following release from works. This line was formerly an important main-line route linking London Paddington with Birmingham/Wolverhampton but by the date of this picture had been reduced in status to a purely local suburban line following the decision to concentrate all traffic between London and the West Midlands on the West Coast Route. Previously, the Birmingham Pullman and restaurant car expresses could be photographed here but by this time a humble DMU was the best that could be seen. *Michael Mensing*

Left: Many places on the railway that were once vital traffic centres or boasted major installations have declined in importance, but Tyseley still retains a large diesel depot servicing units employed throughout the Birmingham area plus, of course, a privately-run steam locomotive works. Needless to say, the station is still very much in business. When this picture was taken in 1964 BR steam traction was still in use at Tyseley but its days were very much numbered. A BR Derby-built three-car unit forming a local service to Birmingham Moor Street is depicted in this illustration, the vehicle nearest to the camera being a driving motor second. The number displayed on a card in the driver's window probably indicates the unit's cyclic working, the purpose of these workings being to ensure that each unit returns regularly to its home depot for fuelling and maintenance. *Michael Mensing*

Some of the rooftops of Frome are just visible on the horizon as Brush Type 2 A1A-A1A No.31 414 regains the main line at Clink Road Junction after making a detour to serve Frome station. The signal box is a real gem and was doubtless a busy spot on summer Saturdays, like all boxes on the main line to the west! The locomotive seen here was originally built as No.D5814 and entered service in September 1961, working at first in the Sheffield area. Note the train's peculiar formation which, in addition to a particularly neglected LMSR full brake (coded BG) marshalled immediately behind the engine, also includes a BR Standard full brake in the middle of the train. Perhaps this was done to give the guard greater visibility at station stops so he could more easily spot any doors left 'on the catch' by negligent passengers – central door locking on trains was still some way off at that time! A June 1979 picture. *Michael Mensing*

BRUSH TYPE 2 A1A-A1A (CLASS 31)

Some railway locations are instantly recognisable, usually due to the shape of the distinctive station roof or unusual track layout, but at Castle Cary it was the signal box (on the extreme left), which had all of the grace and charm of a war-time pill box, that made this station so easy to identify. This rather basic, flat-roofed structure was constructed in 1942 after a German bomb had wrecked much of the layout here, together with the original GWR signal box which doubtless possessed much more architectural merit than its austere Second World War replacement. In this picture Brush Type 2 No.31 419 is depicted easing away from its Castle Cary station stop with the lightweight 4.10pm Bristol (Temple Meads) to Weymouth train on 4th August 1979. Note that the train's formation includes a BR Standard full brake immediately behind the locomotive, so one can only assume a lot of prams or parcels were carried on this line. Castle Cary was once an insignificant wayside station on the West-of-England main line but, following the closure of all the other lines in this part of Somerset, it has become an important railhead for a wide area and has a considerably improved service compared to times past. *Michael Mensing*

BRUSH TYPE 2 A1A-A1A (CLASS 31)

Many of today's diesel locomotive aficionados can hardly contain their excitement when they are hauled by a particularly 'rare' locomotive and one wonders how they would have reacted to the especially rare haulage that was available on the Swindon to Highworth branch in the early 1960s. The branch was closed to passengers on 2nd March 1953 but retained an unadvertised workmen's service for many years, for the benefit of the staff at the BR Swindon locomotive works. Incredibly, on occasions the daily branch passenger train was powered by a 0-6-0 204hp diesel shunter and on 18th June 1962, when this picture was taken, the locomotive working the branch was No.D2195 which was, appropriately, a Swindon works product out-shopped in June 1961. No.D2195 had a brief BR career of only seven years and was later sold to a steel works at Llanelli in South Wales. It was cut-up in September 1981. The workmen's branch service lasted for a few more weeks after this fascinating shot was taken, being withdrawn from 6th August 1962. Even at that late date the former station still retained a GWR seat and running-in board. *Hugh Ballantyne*

204HP SHUNTERS (CLASS 03)

The dying days of the Malmesbury branch. Opened by the Malmesbury Railway on 17th December 1877, the 6½ miles-long branch from Dauntsey, on the Wootton Bassett to Chippenham line, had an interesting history. In 1903 a new route from Wootton Bassett to the Severn Tunnel was opened and this passed over the Malmesbury branch near Little Somerford. In the early 1930s it was decided to lay a connection from Little Somerford to the branch and this was opened from 17th July 1933, from which date the section onwards to Dauntsey was closed. Not many branch lines have had their main-line connection changed from one route to another. The line lost its passenger service from 10th September 1951 but freight traffic continued until 12th November 1962. For most of this period steam traction reigned supreme but for the final two years of the line's existence the goods train was powered by a diminutive 204hp diesel shunter and in this view, taken on 12th June 1962, No.D2187 is seen ticking over amid the ruins of the former Malmesbury station which appears to have taken on the role of an agricultural machinery depot! The old station is prominent on the right of the picture while on the extreme left the decaying engine shed still stands as a reminder of more prosperous times. *Hugh Ballantyne*

The 204hp shunters were certainly not confined to branch lines, and it has to be admitted that the selection of pictures in this section gives a misleading impression – perhaps it was simply the case that these engines were more likely to be photographed on branch line work! Their more usual duties were as yard shunters, especially where tight curvature required the use of a short-wheelbase locomotive. Here, No.D2134 is seen posing at Pomphlett, near Plymouth, in 1971 and clearly its crew were very happy to be photographed. Perhaps it was not quite every day that a photographer turned up to take their picture! No.D2134 was a Swindon product dating from February 1960 and it lasted until July 1976, so it had a relatively fair innings by the standards of this class, some of which lasted only seven years in revenue-earning service. Pomphlett was on the old Plymouth (Friary) to Turnchapel branch which lost its passenger service way back in September 1951; there was never a station at that location. *C. Tretheway/Colour Rail.com*

Saturday 30th December 1967 will be remembered by many enthusiasts as the day steam traction 'finished' at Carlisle, an event which eliminated steam from a large swathe of northern England. In the south-west however, that fateful day will be remembered because it saw the withdrawal *en masse* of the North British Locomotive Co. (NBL) A1A-A1A 'Warship' class that had proved to be one of the most troublesome designs built as part of the modernisation plan. The inspiration for the A1A-A1A and later B-B 'Warships' came from the 'V200s' operating in West Germany and NBL, which already had links with German locomotive manufacturers, was awarded the contract to build five A1A-A1A machines, the first of which appeared in January 1958. These 117-ton locomotives incorporated two NBL/MAN 12 cylinder L12V18/21A 1,000hp engines and, of course, had hydraulic transmission, this being favoured on the WR in contrast to the other BR regions which were standardising on electric transmission. Named after warships, it is perhaps unfortunate that No.D600, the doyen of the class, was named *Active* because this type proved to be one of the most inactive classes produced under the modernisation plan due to constant, inherent unreliability which proved impossible to cure. No.D600 is recorded to have been in Swindon works on 3rd May 1959 when a party from the Railway Correspondence & Travel Society toured the shops and, believe it or not, the locomotive was still there in green undercoat paint when this picture was taken on 28th June. Hopefully, after this length of time the staff had worked out how to put this box of tricks back together. Later in its short career, *Active* was out-shopped from Swindon works in May 1967 in corporate blue livery and was the sole member of its class to sport full yellow ends. Despite this lavish attention, it was taken out of service at the end of that year. *John Langford*

NBL CO. 'WARSHIP' TYPE 4 A1A-A1A (CLASS 41)

Yes, it is working! A westbound express heads towards Reading near Iver on 22nd August 1959 with North British A1A-A1A 'Warship' No.D600 *Active* in command. The locomotive's long sojourn at Swindon during the early summer of 1959 had obviously paid dividends. *Colour Rail.com*

In March 1958 a second member of the A1A-A1A 'Warship' class took to the rails, this being No.D601 *Ark Royal*. Like the other members of the class this locomotive was originally equipped with train classification discs but was later fitted with split box reporting number panels and small yellow warning panels as seen here. This picture was taken at Bodmin Road on 11th June 1966. In their early years these 'Warships' were trusted with some of the most prestigious named expresses on the WR, including the 'Cornish Riviera Express', but by the mid-1960s were largely confined to Cornwall because only crews in the far south-west were conversant with them. In addition, staff at Laira depot understood their idiosyncrasies better than most. *Colin Caddy*

The 'Warships' were nothing if not versatile and proved to be equally at home on both fast passenger and freight haulage. There had been worries that their lightweight construction would provide inadequate brake force for working freight trains but the growth of fully fitted workings alleviated this potential problem. They were robust machines capable of feats of haulage out of all proportion to their modest dimensions and their regular use on heavy stone trains from Merehead quarry to Gatwick Airport bears testament to their abilities. In this view No.D816 *Eclipse* is seen on a much less taxing assignment, working a freight train in Cornwall which includes china clay wagons towards the rear. It was photographed near Fowey on 22nd July 1960. A total of 38 'Warship' Class locomotives (Class 42) were built at Swindon, the remaining 33 being constructed by the North British Locomotive Co. in Glasgow (Class 43). This particular example entered service in February 1960 and survived until September 1972. The Swindon-built production series examples weighed 78 tons and (apart from No.D830 *Majestic* which was fitted with a Paxman engine) had Maybach 650 V-type engines which developed 1,135hp at 1,530 rpm. Three 2,000hp pilot scheme locomotives were ordered as part of BR's supposed evaluation of diesel types but before any of those had turned a wheel a further order was placed for a production series at Swindon with engines of 2,200hp. The first Swindon-built 'Warship' to enter traffic was No.D800 *Sir Brian Robertson*, named after the Chairman of the British Transport Commission, and its inaugural public run took place on 15th July 1958 when it powered the down 'Cornish Riviera Express' from Paddington to Plymouth, returning the following day with the 1.20pm Penzance to Paddington. *R.C. Riley*

BR/NBL CO. 'WARSHIP' TYPE 4 B-B (CLASSES 42 AND 43)

Yes, it is No.D816 again! The 10.10am SuO Wolverhampton to Penzance train, headed by 'Warship' Class B-B No.D816 *Eclipse*, is seen slogging up Dainton bank on 6th August 1961. Passengers travelling throughout on this train were faced with a marathon journey lasting more than ten hours, the advertised arrival time at Penzance being 8.30pm – thankfully a restaurant car was included in the formation. *Hugh Ballantyne*

Familiar location, different angle. Many hundreds of photographs, if not thousands, must have been taken from the conveniently situated overbridge astride Cowley Bridge Junction, on the northern outskirts of Exeter. The most popular view from the bridge is of a southbound train but, when the sun is in the right position, a picture of a northbound working is also possible and, indeed, such a photograph is featured elsewhere in this album. This illustration was taken south of the bridge, however, and shows a southbound express heading towards Exeter St David's station on 5th July 1961 with 'Warship' B-B No.D826 *Jupiter* in charge. Note the carmine and cream coach in the train's formation; this livery was very much 'on the way out' at this time, being superseded by maroon for loco-hauled coaching stock, except on the Southern Region which favoured traditional green livery. *R. C. Riley*

Opposite top: There can be no doubt about the location of this picture nor, indeed, the period during which it was taken. This view of the Royal Albert Bridge, with the road bridge under construction alongside, was taken on 2nd April 1961 and shows an unidentified 'Warship' heading eastwards on an express comprised of a mixture of GWR-designed and BR Standard Mk.1 carriages in chocolate and cream livery. The town of Saltash, on the western shore of the river Tamar, forms the background. Each of the main spans of the railway bridge is 455ft long and has 100ft clearance at high water, this requirement having been stipulated by the Admiralty. The spans were assembled on site and slowly raised by jacks and the whole structure was no doubt regarded as one of the railway wonders of the world at the time of its construction; it was opened in 1859. It was a remarkable engineering achievement and people probably marvelled at such an undertaking. The opening of the road bridge in October 1961 put paid to the Plymouth to Saltash and vice versa auto-train workings that had been a familiar sight for decades. *John Beckett*

Opposite bottom: A down milk empties returning to St Erth hauled by an unidentified 'Warship' is seen near Grafton East Junction on Sunday 27th August 1961. The Andover to Cheltenham former Midland & South Western Junction line crossed over the Berks & Hants line on a bridge near this point and various curves connected the routes. *John Langford*

BR/NBL CO. 'WARSHIP' TYPE 4 B-B (CLASSES 42 AND 43) ─────────────

The WR's express named trains often displayed attractively painted headboards which immediately distinguished them from ordinary passenger workings but the 'Torbay Express' headboard seen here is dull and rather anonymous in comparison ... one could almost say it looks a bit lost on the front of the locomotive. This picture shows a rather grubby No.D807 *Caradoc* hauling a massive fourteen-coach load at Savernake in 1962. *Caradoc* had the third longest innings (13 years 3 months) of any 'Warship' class locomotive. It entered traffic in June 1959 and survived to become one of the final members of the class in service, lasting until withdrawal came in September 1972 – quite an achievement by 'Warship' standards! *Rodney Lissenden*

BR/NBL CO. 'WARSHIP' TYPE 4 B-B (CLASSES 42 AND 43)

Exeter St David's is probably one of the most instantly recognisable stations on the former Western Region and in this view an unidentified down train is seen awaiting departure with 'Warship' Class No.D803 *Albion* in charge on 15th September 1963. The late 1950s/early 1960s was not a happy time for the railway industry which was facing the twin problems of a rapidly spiralling deficit and falling traffic due to intense competition from the growth of private car ownership and the road haulage industry. BR had intended to evaluate small numbers of various designs of diesel locomotives but suddenly decided to place large orders for designs that were totally untried and untested – a policy that, in the case of some classes, proved to be catastrophic. In the event, the Swindon-built 'Warships', despite being ordered straight off the drawing board, acquitted themselves quite well in traffic, their premature demise being caused by their hydraulic transmission which was later deemed to be 'non-standard'. This locomotive was the first of the uprated production series of the class to enter traffic, in March 1959, and its initial home depot was Plymouth (Laira). *Albion* lasted until January 1972 and was eventually cut-up at the place of its birth in October 1972. Like the 'pilot scheme' locomotives, the first ten production series machines were equipped with rather unsightly brackets for displaying stencils that indicated the train reporting number – BR was still very much in the steam age at the time – and these are clearly visible in the picture. Note the two white discs denoting an express passenger train. *Colin Caddy*

A lovely spring evening at Dawlish – 17th May 1964. People stroll along the promenade, a few hardy souls paddle in the water while other, less adventurous, folk merely sit on the sand and enjoy the warm Devon sunshine ... who knows, rain could have been forecast for the following day! Dawlish station is visible on the extreme left as a 'Warship' heads westwards with a down express. In the distant background the estuary of the river Exe can just be discerned while beyond is the eastern shore of the river. Some of the cars parked on Marine Parade would be collectors' items today. *John Beckett*

The second of the production series locomotives was No.D804 *Avenger* and this locomotive is seen here on a down express near Wootton Bassett on 27th September 1964. *Avenger* entered service in April 1959 and remained in traffic until October 1971. This machine was originally equipped with a three-character train describer panel but this had been replaced by a four-character blind display. This picture vividly illustrates how the railway has changed over the intervening years; note the old-fashioned lower quadrant signal with a wooden post, and jointed track with, in the case of the up line, bullhead rail. The lineside vegetation is, however, in a particularly neat and tidy condition that would be hard to find today. *Colin Caddy*

BR/NBL CO. 'WARSHIP' TYPE 4 B-B (CLASSES 42 AND 43)

What a mess! Judging by the disgusting state of its front end, it looks as though 'Warship' B-B No.D860 *Victorious* was suffering from badly flaking paint – hardly a good mobile advertisement for rail travel. Whatever the reason it is to be hoped that No.D860's paintwork was touched up soon after this shot was taken. *Victorious* was working the 9.30am SO Paddington to Paignton on 13th June 1964 and this picture was taken at Taunton station; this train ran only during the height of the summer. Like its sister engines built by the North British Locomotive Company No.D860 proved to be a disastrous investment for the British taxpayer. It entered service in January 1962 and was withdrawn in March 1971 after less than ten years in traffic; it was subsequently cut-up at Swindon in December 1971. *Colin Caddy*

Unlike their Swindon-built counterparts, the 'Warships' constructed by the North British Locomotive Co. (NBL) could not be considered anything approaching a glittering success, largely due to the unreliable MAN engines with which they were equipped. A common fault with these engines was oil leaks, which hardly endeared them to the fitting staff, while the train crews probably disliked them because starting up from cold sometimes generated unhealthy fumes in the cab. Perhaps it is significant that all of the dozen or so 'Warships' that made it into 1972 were Swindon-built examples and many of the NBL locomotives achieved a working life of less than ten years. The locomotive that had one of the worst records of all in this respect was No.D848 *Sultan* which is depicted at Taunton powering the northbound 'Devonian' on 13th June 1964. In fact, No.D848 had a working life of less than eight years, being put into traffic in April 1961, stored unserviceable in February 1969 and withdrawn the following month, when it became one of the first production series locomotives to be condemned with the lowest recorded mileage of just 537,000. One wonders if the long-suffering British taxpayer ever found out about such an appalling waste of money! The small oval-shaped plate to the right of the left hand buffer was peculiar to the NBL-built locomotives and used for affixing the owning depot's shed plate. Another distinguishing feature concerned the lamp brackets and tail lights which were in line on the Swindon-built locomotives but not on the NBL products. *Colin Caddy*

Over the years hundreds of photographs, perhaps thousands, have been taken at locations such as Sonning cutting and alongside the sea wall between Dawlish and Teignmouth but here, for a change, is a picture taken at Somerton, between Castle Cary and Taunton, which is probably one of the least photographed locations on the former WR main lines. The main line from London to the west appears to have been at least partially closed for engineering works on 21st March 1965 when this shot was taken (note the newly laid track in the foreground) and 'Warship' No.D812 *Royal Naval Reserve 1859-1959* stands on the left at the head of a permanent way train while a North British Type 2 is also in attendance. The ruins of the erstwhile Somerton station, which was closed from 10th September 1962, can be seen in the background but the signal box remains very much in use, the line still being semaphore signalled at this time. Note the smoke marks on the bridge which serve as reminders of the steam age. By this date steam traction on the WR was in its death throes and steam workings through Somerton were very likely a thing of the past. *Mike Jose*

The WR hydraulic classes wore a multitude of liveries compared to other types and, perhaps, this is one of the reasons why they were so popular. Maroon was selected for the 'Westerns' as early as 1962 but, for reasons unknown to the author, three years elapsed before the first 'Warship' appeared in this colour, the first example emerging from Swindon in September 1965. Needless to say, none of the D600 series 'Warships' or 'Hymeks' ever appeared in maroon and the repainting of the D800 series in this livery only lasted for about 15 months after which time corporate rail blue was used for all the main line fleet. One of the beneficiaries of an apparent decision to start painting 'Warships' in maroon was No.D812 *Royal Naval Reserve 1859-1959,* the locomotive seen in the previous picture, which was photographed near Frome hauling an unidentified up train on 26th June 1966. It is fair to say that the combination of a maroon locomotive and matching rake of coaches would have looked more in place on the London Midland Region(!), but at least the waist-height yellow destination boards, which were peculiar to the WR, identify it as a WR train.
John Beckett

The history of the Plymouth to Brighton through train can be traced back many years and, of course, this train was traditionally associated with the former 'Southern' route from Plymouth to Exeter via Okehampton, from where it travelled via Salisbury. Sadly, one of the most misguided policies during the Beeching era was the elimination of so-called duplicate routes, and the former SR route was perceived to be in this category despite the undisputed fact that the steeply graded former GWR line, which had an exposed coastal stretch, was vulnerable to disruption during bad weather. The WR decided to dispense with the through route via Okehampton and the first part of the running-down process was the diversion of the more important long distance services, the Plymouth to Brighton train being duly diverted to run via Newton Abbot from March 1967. Just over a year later, on 6th May 1968, the Bere Alston to Okehampton line was closed completely to passengers and Paddington had 'successfully' killed off another former 'Southern' line. In this view the Brighton-bound train is seen near Teignmouth behind No.D817 *Foxhound* on 22nd April 1967, shortly after being transferred to this route. So, rather than admire the wilds of Dartmoor, passengers were treated to extensive sea vistas. No.D817 was later painted with full yellow ends whilst still in maroon livery and was still sporting maroon when it was withdrawn in the major cull of remaining 'Warships' that occurred in October 1971. *Colin Caddy*

A close-up of a nameplate of No.D818 *Glory*. This locomotive survived at Swindon works until it was suddenly dismantled shortly after the public announcement of the closure of the works in 1985. *Ian Foot*

The seaside town of Dawlish is visible in the background as 'Warship' No.D841 *Roebuck* skirts the sea wall with the 10.42am Newton Abbot to Paddington train on 4th September 1971. Note the two small round apertures below the train reporting number panel; this modification was undertaken on numerous North British 'Warships' based at Old Oak Common in an attempt to improve cab ventilation. *Roebuck* was another locomotive condemned in October 1971 as part of the mass slaughter of 'Warships' which eliminated the unreliable North British-built machines. Perhaps it had been fortunate to last that long, being stored for a couple of months in early 1969 and stored unserviceable from November 1969 to June 1970. It was eventually broken-up at Swindon in February 1972. *Nick Tindall*

BR/NBL CO. 'WARSHIP' TYPE 4 B-B (CLASSES 42 AND 43)

The Gloucester RCW Co. constructed a total of 25 'Cross Country' units (plus six spare motor coaches) for use on medium distance services and the first entered traffic in 1958. Here, one of these units heads an eastbound six-coach formation which is seen passing Limpley Stoke, between Bath and Trowbridge, on 6th August 1961. The units were formed of a driving motor brake composite (DMBC), a trailer second lavatory with a small buffet (TSLRB) and a driving motor second lavatory (DMSL). The units provided accommodation for 18 first and 144 second class passengers and it should be noted that the buffet section proved to be uneconomical and all had been taken out of service by the mid-1970s. The units were powered by four 150hp engines and the total weight of each unit was 106 tons. A feature of this stock was the large guard's compartment and very comfortable seating which was designed to compare favourably with the accommodation provided in the loco-hauled trains they were replacing. Some units were sometimes augmented with a GWR Hawksworth composite vehicle modified to operate as a DMU trailer car. *John Beckett*

GLOUCESTER RCW CO. 'CROSS COUNTRY' THREE-CAR UNITS (CLASS 119)

The neatly trimmed cutting-sides and rather dainty GWR fixed-distant signal do not offer much help in identifying where this picture was taken. The location is south of Yeovil Pen Mill station and the train depicted is a Bristol to Weymouth working, the front unit of which is a Gloucester RCW Co. three-car 'Cross Country' set with its DMSL leading . When they were first introduced the vast bulk of these units was based at either Cardiff (Canton) or Bristol, with a few allocated to both Tyseley and Reading depots. The line runs parallel to the Yeovil Town to Yeovil Junction link at this point but this is concealed by the cutting on the left of the shot. South of Castle Cary, where it leaves the main line from Paddington to the West Country, the Weymouth route serves few large intermediate centres of population, apart from Yeovil and Dorchester, both of which are served by direct trains to London on other routes, and it is perhaps fortunate that the line escaped closure in the 1960s. The route was later singled south of Castle Cary, however, in order to reduce maintenance costs. This photograph was taken on 2nd June 1963. *John Beckett*

GLOUCESTER RCW CO. 'CROSS COUNTRY' THREE-CAR UNITS (CLASS 119)

Unlike the location seen in the previous picture this spot is likely to be immediately recognised by many readers because it is one where trains, including DMUs, can still be photographed today. The location is Doniford, on the former Taunton to Minehead branch, which is nowadays operated by the West Somerset Railway (WSR) north of Bishops Lydeard. The picture shows a southbound train approaching the spot where Doniford Halt is now situated – there was never a station here in past times, the halt being built by the volunteers of the WSR. The carriage nearest to the camera is a DMBC which contained 18 first class seats in a saloon located immediately behind the driving compartment. By the time this photograph was taken on 13th June 1970 many of these units were still concentrated at Bristol but some were based at Chester on the LMR. Many units finished their working lives at Reading where their large brake vans made them ideal for use on Gatwick Airport services. *John Spencer Gilks*

GLOUCESTER RCW CO. 'CROSS COUNTRY' THREE-CAR UNITS (CLASS 119)

A damp day at Ledbury. In this classic scene a six-car DMU rake, forming the 11.10am Cardiff General to Birmingham Snow Hill train, pulls out of Ledbury under a blue haze of exhaust fumes and heads for the tunnel at the eastern end of the station. In the centre of the shot former GWR railcar No.W19W, in carmine and cream livery, awaits its next duty on the branch line to Gloucester. This picture was taken on 27th June 1959. The rear unit of the Birmingham working is a Swindon 'Cross Country' three-car set consisting of a driving motor second lavatory (68 seats), trailer second with a lavatory and small buffet (64 seats), and another motor coach plus a brake compartment which contained seats for 18 first and 16 second class passengers. These units had four 150hp engines and weighed a total of 104 tons. The first of this stock appeared in October 1957 and was initially shared between Bristol and Cardiff depots, with the latter having the bulk of the fleet. When construction of the first batch had been completed in early 1959 two further batches were built, one for the Scottish Region, which used the units on the Aberdeen to Inverness line, and another series for use on WR services was built in 1961 (see following illustrations). Unlike most designs of DMU, which had three driver's cab windows, the 'Cross Country' units only had two, giving them quite a distinctive appearance, and were thus easily recognised. This fascinating picture is full of interest – note the gas lighting, neatly tended platform flower display and GWR lower quadrant signals. The goods yard beyond the platform seems to be quite busy with coal traffic and appears to have taken on the guise of a railway museum, with an old coach body and part of the structure of a signal box being visible in the background. *John Langford*

SWINDON-BUILT 'CROSS COUNTRY' THREE-CAR UNITS (CLASS 120)

The Malvern Hills provide a splendid backdrop as a Swindon 'Cross Country' unit rolls into Colwall with (what appears to be) an evening Birmingham Snow Hill to Hereford train, a route with which these sets had a long association. Originally this unit had white-painted domes but by the time of this picture the one seen here appears to have got rather dirty, apart from a small area at the very top. This stock had traditional GWR suspended gangways and screw-link couplings whereas the other Swindon-built sets had Pullman type gangways and buckeye couplings. Rather strangely, in a break from normal practice, the first class accommodation in these units was located in a noisy, vibrating motor coach rather than the trailer which would have provided a much smoother ride and given easy access to the buffet. Note the old GWR lower quadrant signals controlled by the adjacent signal box. *Colour Rail.com*

SWINDON-BUILT 'CROSS COUNTRY' THREE-CAR UNITS (CLASS 120)

One of the later 1961-built series of Swindon 'Cross Country' units pulls out of Evesham station with the 3.35pm Stratford-upon-Avon to Ledbury train, one of a number of irregular local services that connected Stratford-upon-Avon with Evesham and Worcester. This photograph, which was taken in 1962, shows a very busy scene with another train just visible in the up platform, while a former GWR steam locomotive and a 204hp diesel shunter are on the left of the picture. The unit depicted was one of nine delivered with a large four-character headcode panel incorporated in the front end. These units were built without a buffet and had 18 first and 152 second class seats. When they first entered traffic they were based solely at Tyseley but were later allocated to Bristol and Plymouth. *Michael Mensing*

SWINDON-BUILT 'CROSS COUNTRY' THREE-CAR UNITS (CLASS 120)

When asked to nominate their favourite stretch of English railway line most aficionados would probably place the spectacular section between Exeter and Newton Abbot in their top three and for many it would be in the 'No.1' spot. After leaving Exeter the line runs alongside the river Exe for mile after mile and then, from Dawlish to Teignmouth, between the cliffs and sea wall. On a clear day the views across the water towards Exmouth and beyond are absolutely breathtaking. From Teignmouth to Newton Abbot the tracks follow the north bank of the river Teign. In this picture, taken on a sunny 17th May 1964, a Swindon 'Cross Country' unit is seen at Horse Cove on an unidentified westbound working with the town of Dawlish forming the backdrop in the distance. *John Beckett*

Weed infested platform surfaces, boarded-up windows and a down line with very rusty rail surfaces, this was the rather depressing scene at Crowcombe as a six-car DMU ran into the platform on 18th July 1970 with the 2.05pm Taunton to Minehead train. The front unit is one of the later batch of Swindon 'Cross Country' units which were constructed without a buffet but with a standard four character headcode panel that looked rather clumsy and hardly enhanced the unit's front end. The leading coach is a composite with two second class seating bays sandwiched between the first class seating and very large brake van. This was the last summer of BR operations on the line, the passenger service being withdrawn from 4th January 1971. Since this picture was taken, however, Crowcombe station has been lovingly restored and a new signalbox constructed in true GWR style – what a transformation. *Hugh Ballantyne*

Most of the pictures in this part of the book featuring Gloucester single-unit railcars were taken on lines that, regrettably, have long since been closed to ordinary traffic. The Ealing to Greenford link, on the outskirts of west London, is an exception, however, and the following two views illustrate single-unit railcars operating on this somewhat obscure backwater in the late 1950s/early 1960s. Here, in the summer of 1959, an unidentified car is depicted leaving Drayton Green Halt with a train presumably bound for Greenford, rather than Ealing Broadway which is the station shown in the rear destination box. Note the rather fine 'pagoda' waiting shelter and brown painted running-in board – the halt obviously still retained some of the old GWR atmosphere at that time.
Roy Denison collection

Another picture taken on the same line, this time showing a Gloucester railcar pulling away from South Greenford Halt towards Ealing in 1960. Once again, the destination shown is misleading and it can be assumed that the correct destination was only displayed on the front of each train, the crews not bothering to show correct information at both ends of the unit. The halt shown here was opened in September 1926 and the description 'halt' was axed in 1969. The summer 1961 timetable reveals that trains ran at approximately half-hourly intervals during the rush hours while an hourly service was provided during the middle of the day. *Roy Denison collection*

GLOUCESTER RCW CO. SINGLE UNIT RAILCARS (CLASS 122)

An unidentified Gloucester RCW Co. single-unit railcar waits at Much Wenlock some time in the early 1960s. Unlike the Pressed Steel vehicles, which had a standard four-digit route indicator panel mounted above the cab in the roof, these single-unit railcars had a roof-mounted destination blind box and a small route indicator panel under the cab windows. This picture shows the somewhat cumbersome exhaust pipes that joined at the top to form a single exhaust vent, an arrangement that was later modified to two separate outlets. Much Wenlock was originally a through station on the Wellington to Craven Arms line but this was closed beyond this point in December 1951 so it was an early casualty. Latterly the service serving Much Wenlock ran to and from Wellington and the single unit cars were introduced on some services in September 1961 in an effort to reduce operating costs, but this was to no avail and the entire service was withdrawn in July 1962. Perhaps the cars should have been given time to prove their worth. *Colour Rail.com*

Railway photographers flocked to the south Devon banks in steam days but few bothered to visit Brixham, a forgotten outpost that appears to have been little-photographed at any time. The Brixham branch was built solely as a result of the tenacity and determination of one man, R.W. Wolston, a local businessman, who wanted the fishing port to prosper and was prepared to support his aims with considerable financial backing, and it was he who financed the branch's construction. The 2 miles-long branch from Churston, on the Newton Abbot to Kingswear line, opened on 28th February 1868 as a private concern but was sold to the GWR in 1883. Unfortunately, the terminus was inconveniently sited on a hillside above the town and local travellers no doubt found the bus service more suited to their needs. BR endeavoured to reduce costs by introducing diesel units and in this portrait No.W55016 is seen ticking-over at Brixham on a sunny 8th August 1962, during the final full year of operation. Closure came on 13th May 1963 and this little-known branch was erased from the railway map. *W. Potter/R.C. Riley collection*

A blizzard hits the Severn Valley. An unidentified Gloucester single-unit railcar, or driving motor brake second in railwayman's parlance, sets off from Highley on 29th December 1962 with the driver no doubt hoping to reach Bewdley before his train was completely engulfed in snow. This was the last full year of BR passenger trains along the Severn Valley line and the amount of traffic on offer can be gauged from the fact that in the 1961 summer timetable there were only five trains advertised in each direction between Bridgnorth and Shrewsbury; the service south of Bridgnorth was slightly better. Some of those trains were probably formed of GWR railcars but the last of these was withdrawn in October 1962, when single-unit railcars of the type seen here presumably took over. Their reign was short-lived, however, because the line was closed to passengers from 9th September 1963. Note the raft of coal wagons which can just be discerned in the siding on the right, a reminder of prosperous times when Highley was busy with goods traffic. This location is now the site of the Severn Valley Railway's 'Engine House' visitor centre. *Roy Patterson*

GLOUCESTER RCW CO. SINGLE UNIT RAILCARS (CLASS 122)

One of the more obscure passenger branches in southern England was the line from Maiden Newton, on the Weymouth to Castle Cary secondary route, to the quiet coastal town of Bridport. In this illustration a pair of single-unit railcars bounce along with a train from Bridport which is depicted approaching Maiden Newton on 2nd August 1964. The leading vehicle is No.W55015, a Gloucester RCW Co. product dating from July 1958. Twenty of these vehicles were constructed and when first introduced they were based at far-flung depots such as Laira, Tyseley and Reading. These 64ft 6in-long units weighed 36 tons, accommodated 65 second class passengers and were powered by two 150hp engines. Note the rather crude and extremely unsightly exhaust pipes. This vehicle was transferred to Leith depot on the Scottish Region in April 1968 and in September 1971 its seating was removed for the vehicle to be converted to parcels carrying. In September 1983 it underwent further modification to route learning car *Sandra* and was renumbered TDB977177. It was eventually withdrawn from traffic in July 1989 after a very eventful life in a variety of guises and, no doubt, liveries. *John Beckett*

GLOUCESTER RCW CO. SINGLE UNIT RAILCARS (CLASS 122)

45

The beautiful rolling hills of Dorset provide a really splendid background to this shot of a Gloucester single-unit railcar heading away from Maiden Newton towards Bridport on 1st September 1964. This picture shows the other end of one of these cars, without the ugly exhaust pipes. The Bridport branch was dieselised in 1959, from which time steam traction became a thing of the past on passenger work. This scenic byway was tabled for closure in the Beeching report of 1963 but the very narrow roads in this area prevented buses from reaching some of the remote villages served by the line and this true backwater survived until 5th May 1975. *John Spencer Gilks*

GLOUCESTER RCW CO. SINGLE UNIT RAILCARS (CLASS 122)

The 12.52pm Kemble to Cirencester train, formed of AC Cars 4-wheeled railbus No.W79978, leaves Chesterton Lane Halt on 5th August 1963. Amazingly, BR ordered 4-wheeled railbuses from five different manufacturers and these diminutive vehicles operated on four regions, the only exceptions being the North Eastern and Southern regions; many were based in Scotland for use on some of the lightly trafficked lines in that part of the world. No.W79978 entered service in November 1958, had a 150hp engine, weighed 11 tons and could carry 23 second class passengers in each of its two saloons located on either side of the central luggage stowage area. This interesting little contraption was purchased for preservation following its withdrawal from traffic in February 1968. Chesterton Lane Halt was one of a number of similar halts enterprisingly opened by BR in a vain attempt to attract new traffic when the Kemble to Cirencester and Tetbury branches were dieselised in February 1959. Regrettably, despite an increase in takings, this was insufficient to stave off closure and both lines succumbed in April 1964. On 4th April No.W79978 had the rather dubious privilege of forming the final train on the Tetbury branch, which reportedly conveyed a coffin addressed to Doctor Beeching.
Michael Mensing

Following the closure of the Gloucestershire branches mentioned above, No.W79978 was drafted down to the West Country where it is seen at Boscarne Junction on 19th March 1966 after arrival from Bodmin North. The railbus appears to have been employed on a shuttle service that operated from Bodmin North station to a new halt at Boscarne which enabled passengers travelling from Wadebridge to Bodmin General on the old GWR route to reach Bodmin North station and *vice versa*. It has to be said that the vehicle seems to be totally dwarfed by almost everything around it! *Roy Patterson*

The North British Locomotive Company (NBL) was one of the foremost locomotive builders during the steam age and their products could be found on railway systems throughout the world. Sadly, they failed to adapt to the diesel era and their once excellent reputation was tarnished to some degree by a series of diesel classes that proved to be very troublesome in service. The Type 2 B-Bs, the first of which appeared in early 1959, were among the unsuccessful designs produced by NBL, though it is likely that BR's rash decision to order locomotives straight off the drawing board was also to blame. These machines were roughly equivalent to half of the same manufacturer's Type 4 'Warship' locomotives which employed two 1,000hp MAN 12 cylinder L12V18/21A engines, though it should be noted that after the pilot scheme locomotives (No.D6300-05) entered service in early 1959 subsequent examples were fitted with an uprated 1,100hp version. It is remarkable that this class of 58 locomotives was constructed over a four year period, the last to be built entering traffic in late 1962. When new, many of the class were shedded at Laira while other examples were based at Bristol, Newton Abbot and Swindon. In this picture an unidentified member of the class is depicted acting as a pilot locomotive to a 'Warship' Type 4 B-B at Brent in 1959. The pair is in charge of an eastbound express and is seen rounding the sharp curve at the east end of the station. *Ken Wightman/David Clark collection*

7th September 1963 saw the end of passenger traffic on the attractive rural branch which connected Witham, between Frome and Castle Cary, with Yatton, on the main Taunton line south of Bristol. In the summer 1961 timetable only four through trains were advertised along the full length of the line, while some short workings from Yatton terminated at Wells. So, this route is unlikely to have been a money spinner for BR. On the last day steam traction predominated but the 10.49am from Witham produced a North British Type 2 as booked, the locomotive being No.D6353, and the train is depicted entering Wookey station. Other duties performed by the class included clay workings from Meeth and milk trains from Hemyock, while in the London area the class was associated with empty stock workings in and out of Paddington. Note that the crew are displaying an incorrect headcode. *Hugh Ballantyne*

NBL CO. TYPE 2 B-B (CLASS 22)

An unidentified member of the class is seen at the site of the former Somerton station in connection with track relaying on 21st March 1965. Note that the locomotive's own nose-end gangway doors must have been damaged at some stage and replaced with a new set from the stores department that did not quite match the locomotive's livery! But at least this resulted in (what was possibly) a unique split yellow warning panel. The locomotive on the right is 'Warship' Type 4 B-B No.D812 *Royal Naval Reserve 1859-1959*. *Mike Jose*

The history of the 5½ miles-long broad gauge Lostwithiel to Fowey branch can be traced back to 1869 when the line opened for goods traffic, primarily for the conveyance of china clay; passengers were not carried. The branch was closed for a period as a result of rivalry between local railway companies and re-opened as a standard gauge line in 1895 conveying both passenger and goods traffic. The passenger service was withdrawn from 4th January 1965 but china clay trains continued to operate and in this view a pair of unidentified NBL Type 2s working in multiple is depicted passing through the former station at Fowey with a train of empty china clay wagons from the jetties beyond the station. The leading locomotive is in sparkling condition and has clearly just benefited from a trip to Swindon works. Viewed from this angle note the striking resemblance to the NBL A1A-A1A 'Warship' locomotives. *Mike Jose*

A view of Exeter St Davids station on 1st May 1969 showing NBL Type 2 B-B No.D6337 apparently awaiting departure with an unidentified southbound train comprising seven coaches – a fair load for one of these moderately powered locomotives. This class, as previously mentioned, was delivered over a very long period, there being an eight month gap between the delivery of No.D6336 in July 1961 and D6337 which entered service in March 1962. Many representatives of this class were withdrawn while still in green livery, but No.D6337 was privileged, if that is quite the appropriate word, to be repainted in corporate blue, this occurring during a visit to Swindon works in late 1967. This particular locomotive has the numbers above the BR 'double arrow' symbol but later blue repaints had the number below the arrows. No.D6337 survived until October 1971 and was scrapped at Swindon in May 1972. *David Wigley*

NBL CO. TYPE 2 B-B (CLASS 22)

A total of 39 high-density units, plus six spare motor coaches, was constructed in 1959/60 by Pressed Steel (part of the British Motor Corporation) for use on suburban services radiating from Paddington. These 600hp units were formed of a driving motor brake second, trailer composite lavatory and driving motor second which originally provided a total of 24 first and 206 second class seats. Unlike their Derby-built sister units in the West Midlands and South Wales the units employed in the London area at least had toilet accommodation in the trailer car and later all of the units were fitted with a through corridor connection, thus enabling all passengers to access the toilet and the guard to walk through the train checking tickets. It should be noted, however, that the installation of the gangway resulted in a slight reduction in seating capacity. In the early years of this stock the units were

allocated to either Reading or Southall depots and later the vast bulk was concentrated at the former depot with a few vehicles having migrated to either Laira or Tyseley. In this picture a six-car rake of these Pressed Steel units, forming the 4.03pm Paddington to Reading train, is seen entering Maidenhead against the background of a dark sky on 16th May 1965. *Terry Phillips*

One of the benefits of modernisation? A three-car Pressed Steel unit rattles into Paddington station forming a local service in 1961. These units were hardly the last word in passenger comfort and local rush-hour passengers travelling into London must have envied the long-distance commuters who journeyed in the comparative luxury of a Mk.1 loco-hauled carriage. They certainly did not have to tolerate the continuous vibration of the under floor engines, obnoxious fumes entering the passenger saloons or ferocious draughts in wintertime. Lucky old Pewsey commuters! *Colour Rail.com*

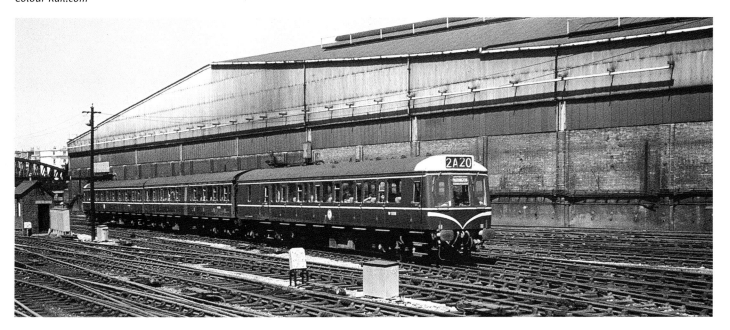

PRESSED STEEL THREE-CAR SUBURBAN UNITS (CLASS 117)

The Maidenhead to Marlow branch is a delightful byway within close proximity to London and in this view a Pressed Steel unit is depicted at Bourne End on 24th June 1961 forming a working to Maidenhead. It should be noted that the identity of this train is uncertain and it may be a working from High Wycombe to Maidenhead, a service that was withdrawn on 4th May 1970. The leading coach is motor brake second No.W51352 which entered service in June 1960 at Reading depot. This vehicle was formed in a unit that later proved to be one of the more nomadic in the fleet. In 1980 it was based at Cardiff and ten years later was in use on services radiating from Birmingham and allocated to Tyseley, so it was certainly widely travelled by the standards of an unpretentious suburban DMU. *John Beckett*

Opposite: Photographed in really soft winter lighting, a Pressed Steel unit is seen in a lovely setting just north of Kings Sutton forming a train to Banbury on 28th January 1967, with the lofty spire of the local church prominent in the background. By this date many units had been repainted in corporate blue livery without any lining and it is very questionable whether the change of livery represented an improvement. These units were outshopped in unlined green when new, before lining became standard in a bid to improve their appearance and, despite the sunshine, the example depicted here looks very drab without lining. Note the tall telegraph poles alongside the tracks, a feature of the railway 'landscape' that has, regrettably, since been confined to history. *John Beckett*

PRESSED STEEL THREE-CAR SUBURBAN UNITS (CLASS 117)

Sunshine and snow – a magic combination. One can almost feel the biting, penetrating cold in this shot of a Pressed Steel unit accelerating away from Goring & Streatley on 12th December 1981. In the background a similar unit can be seen in the platform, presumably forming a London-bound train. This particular unit is No.L418, the letter 'L' denoting the London division. All of the droplights are closed – not surprisingly in view of the artic weather conditions – but one is tempted to ask how cosy the passengers were bearing in mind that this stock, as previously mentioned, was extremely draughty due to the fact that doors were provided to every seating bay. Note this unit is equipped with marker lights, with which all this type were modified as they passed through shops. *Roy Denison*

PRESSED STEEL THREE-CAR SUBURBAN UNITS (CLASS 117)

A total of 183 BR/Sulzer 1Co-Co1 Type 4 production series locomotives was produced plus ten prototype machines which were less powerful and had other detail differences to the main batch. The prototypes were named after mountain summits in England and Wales and the entire class was universally known as the 'Peaks'. The first ten prototypes entered service between April 1959 and February 1960 and were equipped with a Sulzer 12 cylinder 12LDA28-A power plant which produced 2,300hp (one locomotive was rated experimentally at 2,500hp) and the locomotives had six Crompton Parkinson traction motors. Delivery of the 2,500hp production series locomotives started in October 1960 and these had a later, uprated version of the same engine with the same type of motor while a later batch of this class (Nos.D138

to D193) was fitted with Brush traction motors. All of these machines, which were entirely BR-built at Crewe and Derby works, weighed 138 tons 2 cwt so they were quite heavy locomotives. The first recorded appearance of a 'Peak' on the WR occurred on 15th April 1961 when No.D93, which was fresh out of Crewe works, was sent to Bristol St Philip's Marsh depot 'on loan' for running-in and crew training purposes and was reportedly put to work on local passenger and freight duties between Bristol and Gloucester. No.D93 was not destined to stay in the West Country, however, and was later re-allocated to Derby shed but ten sister engines, Nos.D33 to D42, were later permanently based at Bristol. This picture shows 'Peak' No.D27 on the type of cross-country working the class was associated with for many years. It was photographed near the site of the former Droitwich Road goods station, just south of Bromsgrove, working the 1.08pm Leeds City to Cardiff General train on 3rd May 1963. New from Derby works in April 1961 this locomotive was destined to become one of the early casualties, being withdrawn in January 1981. *Michael Mensing*

A Worcester panorama. BR/Sulzer Type 4 No.D30, in very presentable condition, approaches Worcester Shrub Hill station (which is out of sight on the left) with the 7.32am Derby to Bristol Temple Meads train on 1st May 1966. The locomotive leaving the depot is 'Hymek' B-B No.D7026. The tracks on the right lead to Foregate Street station, Great Malvern and Hereford. By the date of this picture steam working on the WR had ceased, hence only a couple of locomotives – a Brush Type 4 and another 'Hymek' – are visible on the shed in the far background. The tower of Worcester cathedral is prominent on the horizon. No.D30 was new in May 1961 and lasted in traffic until July 1987. *Michael Mensing*

On 15th May 1966 the main Bristol to Birmingham line was closed due to engineering work and services were diverted via the former GWR Cheltenham to Stratford-upon-Avon route. In this shot the 9.10am Bristol Temple Meads to Newcastle train, hauled by BR/Sulzer Type 4 No.D74, is seen just south of the site of Laverton Halt, between Toddington and Broadway. Laverton Halt was closed from 7th March 1960, while regular passenger services on this stretch of line ceased altogether from 25th March 1968. No.D74 entered traffic in November 1960 and had quite a reasonable innings, not being withdrawn until April 1987. *Michael Mensing*

A sunny day in Devon. Another panoramic shot but this time showing a totally different scene that the vast majority of readers will instantly recognise. Yes, it is part of the magnificent coastal stretch of line between Dawlish Warren station, which is just visible in the middle distance, and Teignmouth; the estuary of the river Exe provides a distant backdrop. Note the line of camping coaches, which can just be discerned beyond the footbridge, that have doubtless enabled many railway aficionados to stay 'on location' at this classic spot. The train is the 6.28am Leeds to Paignton, hauled by BR/Sulzer Type 4 No.184, and this picture was taken on 6th September 1971. No.184 was formerly No.D184 but by this date BR had decided to drop the 'D' prefix which had been used to differentiate between steam and diesel locomotives, steam traction having bowed out in August 1968. This particular machine, which was out-shopped from Derby works in October 1962, was one of 57 'Peaks' fitted with Brush rather than Crompton Parkinson traction motors and electrical equipment. Many sister engines were stored during the economic recession in the early 1980s, some destined never to re-enter service, but No.184 remained active until withdrawn in September 1984; it was cut-up at Swindon in January 1986. *Nick Tindall*

Cowley Bridge Junction, situated about 1½ miles north of Exeter St Davids station, is the point where the former 'Southern' line to Plymouth via Okehampton branches off the main former GWR Exeter to London route. In times past the Okehampton line provided through routes to resorts on the Atlantic Coast but traffic on these lines, which traversed sparsely inhabited countryside, was seasonal and they were axed in the mid-1960s. Today only the Barnstaple line has a regular passenger service, while trains operate on an occasional basis to Okehampton during the peak summer months. In this picture an unidentified BR/Sulzer Type 4 approaches Cowley Bridge Junction with an express to the Midlands and north of England on 26th September 1974. Note that this example is fitted with a centrally placed headcode panel in contrast to an earlier picture which shows a locomotive with split box panels. The locomotive pictured here is almost certainly one of the later series with Brush traction motors which became known as Class 46. These machines had a single reporting number panel, whereas the earlier locomotives (Class 45s) had either split boxes or two small boxes grouped together in the centre of the nose end. On occasions, however, nose ends were exchanged between locomotives at main works so one can never really be sure! Note the formation of the train which includes a variety of Mk.1 and Mk.2 coaches all in blue and grey livery. The Mk.1 vehicles immediately behind the engine are a composite corridor (CK) and brake composite corridor (BCK), while the following three carriages are non air-conditioned Mk.2 coaches. *John Spencer Gilks*

It is tempting to describe this picture as a 'once in a lifetime opportunity' but, in reality, one wonders how many railway photographers have actually taken a photograph such as this. The scene is the site of Ashchurch station at 8.07pm on 7th June 1977, a day that began full of promise but deteriorated with showers in the afternoon before a late burst of sunshine. Almost unbelievably 'Peak' No.45 020 turned up at just the right time, rushing past at the head of a Penzance to Birmingham New Street train and the photographer probably could not believe his incredibly good fortune. What a stunning gem of a picture! No.45 020 began life as No.D26 in April 1961 and was initially based at Derby shed, finishing its career at nearby Toton in December 1985. It was eventually scrapped at Vic Berry's, Leicester, yard in July 1988. *Michael Mensing*

BR/SULZER TYPE 4 1Co-Co1 'PEAK' (CLASSES 45 AND 46)

Photographed in soft evening light, 'Peak' No.45 039 *The Manchester Regiment,* hauling what appears to be a parcels train, slowly comes round the curve at the approach to Plymouth in the summer of 1977. This locomotive was formerly No.D49 and one of a number named in the early to mid-1960s, this particular specimen being bestowed with a name in October 1965. It was among a sizeable number of 'Peaks' put into storage in late 1980 due to a decline in traffic as a result of the economic recession and became one of the first of the class to be withdrawn, in December 1980. It was eventually broken-up at Swindon works in the spring of 1983. *Ian Foot*

The Blue Pullman trains, constructed by Metropolitan-Cammell in Birmingham, were conceived as part of the 1955 Modernisation Plan to compete with the private motor car and developing domestic air travel. The 90mph units, which were painted in a striking Nanking blue livery with white window surrounds, set a new standard of luxurious rail travel, with armchair-type seating at tables complete with a table lamp and an adjacent button to summon a steward. The entire train was air conditioned with automatic humidity control, had special sound insulation, and a particularly novel feature was the Venetian blinds between the panes of the double glazed windows. A nice decorative embellishment was the Pullman crests on the front ends and sides of the cars. The first set appeared for trials in October 1959 and the inaugural run was made on the London Midland Region between Manchester Central and London St Pancras via the Peak route in July 1960. The first passenger-carrying journeys on the WR took place on 12th September 1960 and initially the units were confined to two routes, the 'Birmingham Pullman' operating between Wolverhampton Low Level and Paddington while the 'Bristol Pullman' ran between Bristol Temple Meads and Paddington; later the 'South Wales Pullman' operated from Cardiff and Swansea to Paddington. The WR units consisted of eight coaches with a mix of first- and second-class accommodation, giving a total of 228 seats. The trains were powered by two NBL/MAN 1,000hp engines which provided power for eight 425hp traction motors fitted to four vehicles in the train. Unfortunately the units had an achilles heel, this being their tendency for rough riding at speed and this problem was never really cured. Here, the 4.50pm Paddington to Wolverhampton Low Level train is seen near Acocks Green, in the Birmingham suburbs, on 27th June 1961.
Michael Mensing

The Blue Pullman is seen again, this time in the magnificent surroundings of Paddington station as it was in 1965 with maroon coaching stock and green-liveried diesel units. The completion of the West Coast Main Line (WCML) electrification in 1966 revolutionised rail travel between London and Manchester and the Blue Pullman units working on the LMR suddenly lost their appeal, being transferred to the WR in 1967. By this time the 'Birmingham Pullman' had also been made redundant by the WCML electrification and the fleet was put to use on new out-and-back services from Paddington to Oxford, Bristol and Swansea. *Roy Denison*

In 1967 all of the units were robbed of some of their character when mandatory full yellow ends were applied for safety reasons and their appeal was further eroded when, in about 1970, they were repainted in grey and blue livery – the reverse of the standard colour scheme. The two six-car units moved from the LMR had some of their seating downgraded to second class and were fitted with multiple unit jumper cables to enable them to operate as a twelve-coach formation. They are seen here leaving Twerton tunnel near Bath on a gloomy 8th July 1971. The cost of maintaining this small and unique fleet was considerable and many travellers no doubt preferred the Mk.2 air-conditioned stock that was coming on stream at that time, for which no supplement was charged. In addition the Inter-City 125 units were on the horizon. The appeal of the Blue Pullman units was fading rapidly and this, together with the poor riding qualities previously mentioned, meant that the writing was on the wall for this stock. All the Pullman units were withdrawn *en masse* in May 1973 after a very short working life and none survived into preservation. *Mike Jose*

Single-unit railcar No.W55034, in blue livery with a small yellow warning panel, waits to leave Cadoxton with the 1.45pm train to Penarth on 8th April 1967. This service was destined to last for only another year after this picture was taken, being withdrawn from 6th May 1968. No.W55034 was built by Pressed Steel and entered traffic in January 1961; it could seat 65 second class passengers and weighed 37tons 8cwt. In 1986 it was transferred to the London Midland Region and in October 1992 ceased regular passenger operation; it was converted for Sandite use, being renumbered ADB977828. Sandite is a substance that is applied to the rail surface during the leaf fall season to assist adhesion. This railcar was finally withdrawn in June 1996 after a long career and subsequently survived into preservation. At the time of writing it is, however, on hire to Chiltern Railways numbered 55034 and painted BR green, so it is a remarkable survivor. *Terry Phillips*

Opposite top: The same train is seen again, exactly a year earlier, formed of No.W55026, which is depicted leaving Alberta Place Halt *en route* for Penarth. The very short platforms there were just suited to a single unit railcar! Note the small number of cars on the adjacent residential roadway – today parking places are no doubt at a premium. *Hugh Ballantyne*

Opposite bottom: Photographed from a strategically positioned road bridge, the 9.04am Severn Beach to Bristol Temple Meads train emerges from Clifton Down tunnel and is about to call at Clifton Down station, located on the other side of the bridge. The single-unit railcar forming the train is No.W55035, one of a series constructed by Pressed Steel Co. Note the unusual position of the up home signal on the opposite side of the track to which it refers; this was presumably done to improve sighting of the signal for drivers. Also worthy of attention is the train reporting number, 1F32 (indicating a Class 1 train), which appears to be a trifle optimistic for a suburban branch line stopping service! This shot was taken on 15th August 1970. *Hugh Ballantyne*

PRESSED STEEL SINGLE UNIT RAILCARS (CLASS 121)

The English Electric Type 3 locomotives were undoubtedly one of the success stories of the BR modernisation plan, a very reliable and versatile design that has really stood the all-important test of time – some examples can still be seen on the main line system today, more than fifty years after the first one made its debut. A total of 309 locomotives was constructed by English Electric (Vulcan Foundry) and Robert Stephenson & Hawthorns, Darlington, and the first one entered service at Stratford shed, East London, in December 1960 while the final machine went into traffic in November 1965. The 108-ton (with variations) locomotives were fitted with an English Electric 12CSVT engine which produced 1,750hp and were capable of speeds up to 90mph. They were very versatile machines which have become one of the longest surviving diesel types and were particularly associated with the West Highland line in Scotland, services in East Anglia and, on the Western Region, trains on the Crewe to Cardiff and Central Wales lines. In addition they were widely used on coal trains and heavy steel workings from the Llanwern steel plant in South Wales. They also operated on the Cambrian lines and in this view an unidentified member of the class is depicted powering up the 1 in 56 gradient towards the summit at Talerddig, on the Cambrian main line, in August 1966, with the deafening noise from the locomotive shattering the peace of this delightful rural area. The train is believed to be a summer Saturday Barmouth to Manchester Piccadilly working. *Author*

ENGLISH ELECTRIC TYPE 3 Co-Co (CLASS 37)

An unidentified English Electric Type 3 in quite presentable external condition leaves Tenby with, reportedly, a rake of empty coaching stock destined for Swansea. Some of these excellent machines were extensively refurbished in the 1980s and this probably accounts for their longevity. This photograph was taken on 19th August 1978. *John Spencer Gilks*

ENGLISH ELECTRIC TYPE 3 Co-Co (CLASS 37)

Strangely, few pictures taken in Wales were submitted for inclusion in this album but here is a shot of a train in the landscape in west Wales on the line between Fishguard and Swansea. Note how the railway, river and road run side by side at this point. An eastbound train hauled by an unidentified Class 37 is depicted near Wolf's Castle on 23rd May 1979 and the train is approaching the 1 in 110 climb up to Spittal tunnel and Clarbeston Road. There used to be a small halt at Wolf's Castle but it was closed from 6th April 1964. *John Spencer Gilks*

A number of DMU parcels vans, officially known as driving motor parcels vans, were produced, the example seen here, No.W55993, being one of six similar vehicles in the W55991 to W55996 series constructed for the WR by the Gloucester Railway Carriage & Wagon Company; other cars were built by Cravens. This 64ft 6in long, 41 ton vehicle was introduced in January 1960 and powered by two 230hp engines and was capable of hauling a 64-ton tail load. Three sets of sliding doors were provided to facilitate rapid loading and unloading. Unlike most parcels vans these particular vehicles had a corridor connection at each end which hardly enhanced their appearance but, in addition, one end also had two engine exhaust pipes and is unlikely to have won accolades from the Design Panel. Some vans of this type were built for the LMR with a corridor connection, but this feature was later removed. This picture was taken near Spring Road, near Acocks Green on the Birmingham to Stratford-upon-Avon line, in 1961.
Michael Mensing

In June 1959 BR placed with Beyer Peacock an order for 45 Type 3 diesel hydraulic locomotives which were to be constructed at the firm's Gorton, Manchester, works. In July 1960 the order was increased to 95 machines and a further six were added later bringing the total to 101. The first member of the class, No.D7000, was ceremonially handed over to BR at Paddington station on 16th May 1961 and the locomotive later entered traffic at Bristol Bath Road depot. The stylish 1,700hp 'Hymeks', as they were universally known, were powered by a Bristol Siddeley/Maybach MD870 engine and had a maximum speed of 90mph. Unlike other hydraulic classes that were a miserable failure the 'Hymeks' were well-liked by enginemen and could be considered the most successful of the diesel hydraulic types. They were quite versatile locomotives and could be found on a wide variety of duties ranging from express passenger workings to short goods trains. A route that enjoyed a long association with the 'Hymeks' was the Paddington to Worcester line and in this illustration an unidentified, but nicely turned out, example is seen approaching Blockley station, between Honeybourne and Moreton-in-Marsh, with a Worcester to London train on 14th September 1963. The station seems to have been kept in spotless condition and oozes Great Western atmosphere with its typical signal box and lower quadrant signals but, even so, Blockley was closed to passengers on 3rd January 1966. *John Spencer Gilks*

BEYER PEACOCK TYPE 3 B-B 'HYMEK' (CLASS 35)

A delightful scene photographed on a summer's evening in rural Herefordshire on 1st June 1963. In this illustration 'Hymek' B-B No.D7076, hauling the lightweight 6.05pm Hereford to Paddington, has just left Ledbury tunnel and heads for its next station stop, presumably at Great Malvern. It would be likely that further coaches were attached to this train at Worcester (Shrub Hill), bearing in mind it would have been scheduled to call at busy stations such as Oxford and Reading. No.D7076, which was only a month old at the time of this photograph, led a charmed life following withdrawal from traffic in May 1973 after exactly ten years service. It was acquisitioned by the Railway Technical Centre at Derby, where no doubt somebody in high places had a soft spot for 'Hymeks', but it apparently was idle for most of the time at the Old Dalby test centre. Another ten years elapsed before No.D7076 was acquired by a group based on the East Lancashire Railway at Bury and it is currently operational after extensive restoration. A lucky locomotive! *Michael Mensing*

A 'Hymek' in the delightful Golden Valley. In the author's opinion one of the loveliest stretches of line on the former GWR is the section between Stroud and Sapperton through the Golden Valley. Here an unidentified 'Hymek' is depicted climbing up to the summit at Sapperton tunnel near Brimscombe on 22nd August 1964 with the infant waters of the tranquil river Frome in the foreground. At the time of this photograph the valley was still served by a steam-operated auto-train service which stopped at local stations between Gloucester and Chalford but this had already been sanctioned for closure and was withdrawn in November 1964, leaving only the main line trains which still called at Stroud. At this time the 'Hymeks' worked both local and through London trains but the service later suffered mixed fortunes, with most workings being replaced by DMUs which terminated at Swindon; in more recent years, however, the pattern of services has improved.
Roy Denison

The 'Atlantic Coast Express', first introduced in 1926, became one of the most famous trains in the south of England due to the many separate portions it conveyed and very demanding schedule; in the early 1960s it was booked to run the 83 miles from Waterloo to Salisbury in an exhilarating 80 minutes. When the WR assumed control of the SR lines west of Salisbury it soon became clear that the role of the Waterloo to Exeter line would be reduced and the route dieselised without delay. In August 1964 'Warship' diesels appeared for the first time east of Exeter on the 'ACE', as the 'Atlantic Coast Express' was known colloquially, while west of Exeter 'Hymeks' had taken over the working of at least some of the portions and in this shot the Ilfracombe portion is seen climbing Mortehoe bank, north of Barnstaple, with an unidentified 'Hymek' at the head of the train. The photographer noted that Maunsell N Class No.31837 was providing rear-end assistance up the 1 in 40 gradient but, apparently, failed to record the number of the diesel so there is no doubt where his allegiance lay! Somehow a WR 'Hymek' diesel locomotive just does not seem fitting motive power for such a prestigious 'Southern' train. *Alan Reeve*

BEYER PEACOCK TYPE 3 B-B 'HYMEK' (CLASS 35)

A clear blue south Devon sky. One can only imagine the deafening noise being emitted by 'Hymek' B-B No.D7029 as it climbs the 1 in 60 incline over Broadsands viaduct between Paignton and Kingswear; the locomotive was working a Cardiff to Kingswear train on 1st October 1964. One is almost tempted to suggest that this picture could still be taken today because this section of line is preserved and No.D7029 also survived into preservation after becoming one of the last active 'Hymeks' in traffic. It lasted until February 1975, being withdrawn just a few weeks before its last sister engines were taken out of service; today it can be seen on the Severn Valley Railway. Note (what appears to be) Churston station's fixed distant signal, complete with an unsightly concrete post, on the right. *Colour Rail.com*

The running-in board on the right of the picture leaves one in no doubt regarding the location of this photograph. Bath Green Park station was the northern terminus of the much-loved Somerset & Dorset line (S&D) which ran up from the south coast at Bournemouth and crossed the Mendip hills before reaching Bath. The S&D remained exclusively steam-worked, apart from the very occasional seasonal DMU working on excursion trains, and the author cannot recall ever seeing a photograph of an ordinary diesel-hauled train on the main part of the S&D, except for the demolition trains. S&D trains destined for Bristol reversed at Bath and diesel traction was often employed on the final part of the run, this becoming more common as the elimination of steam gathered pace. In this picture 'Hymek' B-B No.D7023 pulls out of Green Park station with an afternoon train to Bristol in December 1965 and the steam visible at the far end of the train beneath the overall roof leaves no doubt that the train had been brought up from Bournemouth by steam traction. The listed station building and roof still exist as part of a supermarket complex, but the same cannot be said of No.D7023 which was withdrawn after a working life of just over eleven years in May 1973 and subsequently scrapped at Swindon two years later. *Mike Jose*

BEYER PEACOCK TYPE 3 B-B 'HYMEK' (CLASS 35)

71

The 'Hymeks', as previously mentioned, were quite versatile machines and could be seen on a wide range of duties. Here, No.D7044 hauling a reasonably heavy freight working, has just passed Fairwood Junction and heads for Westbury; the cut-off line avoiding the station is on the left of the picture. The junction takes its name from a tiny hamlet half a mile to the north. The mixed consist of the train includes bitumen tank wagons, presumably from Cranmore. This scene was recorded on 12th July 1969. Note the attractive signal box and lower quadrant signals in the background. *Hugh Ballantyne*

A non-standard, but very pleasing paint job. When the painters at Swindon finished off the first 'Hymek' in all-over blue, including the window frames, not surprisingly it was decided that the new livery was not a patch on two-tone green. In a commendable attempt to brighten-up the appearance of these locomotives it was agreed that the window frames would be painted white (actually 'off white'), thus setting a precedent that other depots, notably Finsbury Park, would follow in later years. One of the beneficiaries of this enlightened decision was No.D7046, seen here at Reading, which by the time of this picture had lost its 'D' prefix. Full marks to Swindon. *Colour Rail.com*

An unidentified 'Hymek' passes the remains of Somerton station with a short freight train on 17th July 1971. The last 'Hymek' entered traffic in February 1964 and it is sad to reflect that the first was withdrawn two months after this picture was taken and less than eight years after the last one was delivered. In October 1971 a sizeable batch of 'Hymeks' was condemned as part of a major cull of the hydraulic classes. The following year saw no fewer than 62 of these locomotives withdrawn from service but after that time the speed of withdrawals slowed considerably, the final survivors lasting until the spring of 1975. *Mike Jose*

Trains running between Cardiff and Portsmouth pass through the Wylye valley which is situated between Warminster and Wilton, and the scenic qualities of the chalk downland on this stretch of line are exemplified here in this shot of a 'Hymek' near Hanging Langford. The train was a Cardiff to Portsmouth Harbour working and this picture was taken on 19th August 1972. The length of this train will be noted – at that time there were probably only half a dozen trains a day between the two cities in contrast to the hourly service that is on offer today using three-car diesel units. There is a string of small villages throughout the length of the valley and some were served by wayside stations, but these obviously produced insufficient traffic to justify their retention and were closed in September 1955. Purists may argue that this illustration does not qualify for inclusion in this book because at the time of the picture this section of line was administered by the Southern Region. The Westbury to Salisbury line was, however, built by the GWR and the motive power is most definitely a WR type which, in the author's view, justifies its inclusion. *John Spencer Gilks*

The Sulzer Type 2 Bo-Bo locomotives were not particularly associated with the WR and as a result few pictures of the class at work were submitted for publication in this album. A total of 327 of these 1,250hp machines was produced between 1961 and 1967, the bulk being constructed by BR at their Darlington and Derby workshops, while a small batch of the later locomotives was built by Beyer Peacock & Co. These locomotives had a 6LDA28-B engine, weighed 71 tons (with variations) and possessed a top speed of 90mph. The class was quite widespread across the BR network but the Southern Region never had an allocation while the WR only had a few. A large number of the class was concentrated in the East Midlands, particularly at Toton and Derby. In the early 1980s the class could be found on Crewe to Cardiff passenger work but they are, perhaps, best remembered for their use on summer Saturday trains to Aberystwyth which, by the modest standards of this class, were quite long-distance, and relatively arduous, workings. In this illustration an unidentified member of the class, hauling an empty ballast train, is seen passing Cowley Bridge Junction, north of Exeter St David's, where the former SR line to Barnstaple branches from the main Exeter to London route. What a pity this otherwise attractive photographic location was dominated by a huge electricity pylon and giant-size telegraph pole – the authorities never seem to take on board the requirements of the railway photographic fraternity! Note the foaming waters of the river Exe on the extreme left of the picture rushing down a series of cascades; this must have been quite a noisy spot for signalmen working in the adjacent box especially when the river was in spate. This picture was taken on 26th September 1974. *John Spencer Gilks*

BR/SULZER TYPE 2 Bo-Bo (CLASS 25)

The order for 74 Type 4 diesel-hydraulic locomotives, that were later to become universally known as the 'Westerns', was placed by the British Transport Commission (BTC) in September 1959 just before the finishing touches had been put to the final design. Construction was to be divided between Swindon and Crewe works and, following a change of plan, Swindon eventually constructed Nos. D1000 to D1029 while Crewe built the lion's share, Nos. D1030 to D1073. The 2,700hp locomotives were powered by two MD655 Maybach V12 65-litre engines, each producing 1,350hp at 1,500 revolutions per minute; the hydraulic transmissions were supplied by Voith. In 1956 the BTC had appointed a design panel to advise on the best way to attain the highest design standards and the panel commissioned one of the most respected teams available, the London-based Design Research Unit (DRU) which was headed by Sir Misha Black. It was his radical approach to rolling stock design that resulted in the stylish and very attractive front-end and he also suggested the use of stainless steel numerals and aluminium crests. It should be pointed out, however, that much of the design work has since been credited to John Beresford-Evans who was a member of the team at the DRU. A debate ensued about the livery to be adopted and some of the rather conservative WR managers at Paddington felt there was no need to depart from the standard locomotive green, but at least some latitude was allowed and the prototype locomotive, No.D1000 *Western Enterprise,* was released in a warm fawn/grey livery that had apparently originally been proposed for the 'Deltics' by a member of the BTC's Design Panel. The name of the fawn colour was 'desert sand' and this livery was subsequently universally known by that name. No.D1000 was officially released to traffic in December 1961 and allocated to Plymouth (Laira) depot. *Western Enterprise* is depicted here posing at Swindon works on 1st July 1962. Note the aluminium emblem, reportedly supplied by the stores department at Derby works which kept a supply for use on London Midland Region electric locomotives! *Colin Caddy*

BR/MAYBACH TYPE 4 C-C 'WESTERN' (CLASS 52)

A green-liveried 'Western' in practically mint condition. The first locomotive to be out-shopped from Crewe works was No.D1035 *Western Yeoman*, this locomotive being released to traffic in July 1962 and allocated to Laira shed. Here, *Western Yeoman* is depicted in sparkling condition near Aynho Junction, south of Banbury, working the 11.40am Birkenhead (Woodside) to London Paddington on 29th August 1962. It was originally planned that 'Western' Class locomotive Nos.D1000 to D1034 would be built at Swindon while Nos.D1035 to D1073 were scheduled to be constructed at Crewe works. No.D1000 was delivered later than had been anticipated and it was decreed that, in order to relieve pressure on Swindon works, Nos.D1030 to D1034 would be built at Crewe instead. This batch of five machines was the last to be constructed by Crewe but No.D1029 *Western Legionnaire*, a Swindon-built example, proved to be the final 'Western' to enter service, an event which occurred in July 1964, so the number series certainly does not give any indication of the order in which the locomotives were delivered. *Michael Mensing*

BR/MAYBACH TYPE 4 C-C 'WESTERN' (CLASS 52)

The records reveal that 'Western' C-C locomotive No.D1001 *Western Pathfinder* entered traffic in February 1962 but there is no doubt that when it was photographed at Taunton seven months later it was still in absolutely pristine condition and it appears that special efforts were being made to keep the yellow buffer beam clean – not an easy task. It was working the 10.15am Paddington to Minehead on 8th September 1962; No.D1001 would have been detached there in favour of a smaller machine as 'Westerns' were barred from the Minehead branch. Only ten 'Westerns' appeared with the very distinctive yellow buffer beams and most of them ran in this condition for only a short time, having the buffer beams repainted black and standard small yellow panels applied to the cab ends after about four months; these locomotives being Nos D1001, D1005–D1009 and D1039–D1042. *Western Pathfinder* was an exception, however, and lasted in this livery until mid-October 1962. Sadly, No.D1001 was destined to meet a grisly end when, in the early hours of 3rd October 1976, it was in collision with an engineer's van on a farm crossing near Stoke Canon, north of Exeter, while powering the previous night's 11.15pm Paddington to Penzance newspaper train. At that time the class was in its death throes and *Western Pathfinder* was immediately withdrawn and broken-up at Swindon almost a year later. *Colin Caddy*

BR/MAYBACH TYPE 4 C-C 'WESTERN' (CLASS 52)

During the summer of 1962 crew training on the 'Westerns' began in the West Midlands prior to their introduction on the Paddington to Wolverhampton main line and it was reported that locomotives worked local trains to and from Stourbridge (which does not sound too strenuous) and the 4.53pm Wolverhampton to Chester and 9.45pm back. The first day of full diesel working was Monday 10th September and the inaugural services at both ends of the route were given a civic send-off. In the down direction the 9.00am from Paddington was seen off by the Mayor of the Borough and arrival at Birmingham (Snow Hill) was seven minutes early, the locomotive being No.D1038 *Western Sovereign*. In the reverse direction the 7.10am from Shrewsbury, headed by No.D1039 *Western King*, was apparently driven by the Mayor of Shrewsbury as far as Birmingham where the Mayor of Birmingham entered the cab for the run to Leamington, the arrival in London being on time. Unfortunately, the gremlins struck the 11.00am from Snow Hill, a trip set aside for the press which was affected by an earlier signal failure at Wednesbury, north of Birmingham, and suffered further delay following the failure of a preceding train at Leamington Spa, and it arrived at Paddington twenty minutes late behind No.D1000 *Western Enterprise*. Despite all the excellent timekeeping by the remainder of the trains, predictably it was the lateness of the 11.00am that grabbed the newspaper headlines the following morning. Nos.D1038 and D1039 had been in traffic only a few days following release from Crewe works so no doubt a fitter travelled on both locomotives in case anything went awry. In this picture No.D1008 *Western Harrier* is seen approaching Acocks Green station with the up 'Cambrian Coast Express' on 17th September 1962, exactly a week after the new service was introduced. *Michael Mensing*

BR/MAYBACH TYPE 4 C-C 'WESTERN' (CLASS 52)

Yes, it is No.D1035 *Western Yeoman* again, but who could resist including this lovely picture of this locomotive powering the up 'Cambrian Coast Express'. This shot was taken in soft autumn light near Acocks Green on 17th October 1962 – the shadows are lengthening but have only just reached the track upon which the train is travelling. This locomotive ran in green livery with small yellow warning panels until November 1965 when it was repainted in maroon, again with small yellow panels. In February 1970 it succumbed to blue livery with full yellow ends, was repainted at Laira in November 1973, and ran in blue until January 1975 when it was withdrawn from traffic. No.D1035 lay out of service for many months before it was eventually cut-up at Swindon in September 1976. *Michael Mensing*

The winter of 1962/63, one of the coldest in living memory, was characterised by sub zero temperatures which lasted for many weeks and most of Great Britain was carpeted by deep snow. It was a particularly trying time for BR, many of whose newly-introduced diesel locomotives were out of action for long periods, a principal fault being train heating boilers that had frozen-up in the bitter conditions. So, even if a diesel locomotive could actually haul a passenger train it would be unable to heat it and steam locomotives had to be substituted with a predictably dire effect on timekeeping. In this picture the 1.00pm Birmingham (Snow Hill) to Paddington 'Birmingham Pullman' train has just passed Acocks Green behind 'Western' Class Type 4 No.D1046 *Western Marquis* on 7th January 1963 at the height of the 'big freeze'. This train was booked to be formed of a diesel Pullman set but perhaps it, too, was 'stopped' out of traffic due to the inclement weather. The photographer comments that he had noticed the diesel Pullman set was out of service a few days previously and he took this shot in his lunch hour which, on that day at least, was put to excellent use! *Michael Mensing*

A unique locomotive that hardly requires identification. No.D1000 *Western Enterprise* is depicted racing through Hayes & Harlington in charge of the 6.30am Plymouth to Paddington train on 27th April 1963. Small yellow warning panels had been applied to No.D1000 in November 1962 and it continued to run in desert sand livery until early October 1964 when it emerged from Swindon works in maroon livery but still with small yellow warning panels. It underwent yet another change of livery in June 1967, being repainted blue with full yellow ends, and it remained in these colours until withdrawn in February 1974, by which time its blue paint must have deteriorated markedly and one wonders whether any of its previous liveries were visible. Note that No.D1000 ran without small brake reservoir hoses on the front shrouds until September 1963 and was the only 'Western' without this feature. *Roy Denison*

BR/MAYBACH TYPE 4 C-C 'WESTERN' (CLASS 52)

When a new General Manager took over at Paddington in 1962 he decreed that all of the 'Westerns' should be painted in maroon livery but it was decided that one exception could be made which involved an idea from the late Brian Haresnape, a graphic designer and railway author. He suggested that a locomotive should be painted in golden ochre, an idea that was readily agreed by Sir Misha Black who (as already mentioned) was head of the Design Research Unit. Brian Haresnape travelled to Derby works to help choose the mix of paints – diesel piping orange and standard WR chocolate brown – that would produce the shade required. It was decided that locomotive No.D1014 *Western Leviathan* would receive the livery but in the event No.D1015 *Western Champion* emerged from Swindon works in this very distinctive colour and, being unique, immediately became something of a celebrity machine. Note the non-standard yellow warning panel that has 'angled' corners and a golden ochre strip at the bottom. No.D1015 wore this livery from January 1963 until its first repaint in November 1965 when it was repainted in maroon with small yellow panels and consequently lost its individuality. *Western Champion* is seen here taking the 12.10pm Paddington to Birkenhead (Woodside) express up the 1 in 110 gradient of Hatton bank, between Leamington Spa and Birmingham, in May 1963. Perhaps the photographer was present to photograph steam traction labouring up the bank but some people might say that a picture of a unique 'Western', in golden ochre livery, was almost as good. Well, almost. *Peter Hughes/Colour Rail.com*

The up 'Cambrian Coast Express' is depicted approaching Acocks Green station with Type 4 C-C 'Western' Class No.D1019 *Western Challenger* in charge on 31st May 1963. The locomotive is hauling a massive 14-coach load comprised mostly of BR Standard carriages, but including a few pre-nationalisation strengthening vehicles immediately behind the engine and, possibly, one or two almost out of sight at the rear of the train. Note the pair of vintage GWR lower quadrant signals both of which have wooden posts. The 'Cambrian Coast Express' was a train with a long history that can be traced back to 1927 when it was introduced by the GWR; at that time it ran only on Fridays and Saturdays and left London at 10.00am. This famous train ceased operation in March 1967 when London to Birmingham services were largely concentrated on the West Coast Main Line and the Paddington to Birmingham (Snow Hill)/Wolverhampton (Low Level) line was downgraded as a result, with all through expresses to Birkenhead and the Welsh coast being withdrawn. *Western Challenger* was destined to have an exceptionally short working life of only ten years. It was out-shopped from Swindon in May 1963 and became one of the last 'Westerns' outstanding for conversion to air braking when four 'Westerns' were deemed surplus to traffic requirements. It was withdrawn in May 1973 thus acquiring the dubious distinction of being among the first of its class to be condemned. *Michael Mensing*

BR/MAYBACH TYPE 4 C-C 'WESTERN' (CLASS 52)

It is the 'Cambrian Coast Express' again, but this time the down train which is seen approaching Tyseley behind 'Western' Class Type 4 No.D1065 *Western Consort* on 15th August 1963. In addition to a fine array of lower quadrant signals the North Warwickshire line can be seen diverging to the right. This used to be part of a through route to Cheltenham Spa via Winchcombe but passenger trains now only operate as far as Stratford-upon-Avon. The 15th August 1963 was a very sad day for railwaymen especially in the West Midlands because three of their colleagues lost their lives in a collision at Knowle & Dorridge between a goods train and a 'Western' Class locomotive which was hauling a spare set of cars on the 'Birmingham Pullman' service as a substitute for a diesel Pullman multiple unit. The men were travelling in the cab of No.D1040 *Western Queen* which was severely damaged in the incident. *Michael Mensing*

The 2.30pm Paddington to Penzance train, with 'Western' C-C No.D1071 *Western Renown* in command, sweeps into Exeter St David's station on 12th September 1964. A maroon-liveried locomotive and a complete set of maroon Mk.1 coaches – one is left to wonder what happened to the WR's 'chocolate and cream' image! At least the running-in board on the right is in the 'correct' colour. No.D1071 was one of the last 'Westerns' to enter traffic, an event which occurred following its release from Crewe works in November 1963; it was initially based at Old Oak Common shed. *Western Renown* lasted in service until almost the end of the class, being withdrawn in December 1976. A further two years elapsed before it was cut-up at Swindon. *Colin Caddy*

BR/MAYBACH TYPE 4 C-C 'WESTERN' (CLASS 52)

Photographed in really lovely spring sunshine, an unidentified 'Western' approaches the western end of Somerton tunnel with (what appears to be) the 9.30am Plymouth to Paddington train on 21st March 1966. The tunnel is located west of Somerton in a rural location, the line being on a rising gradient of 1 in 264 at this point and the locomotive would probably have been working reasonably hard, so the photographer would have had plenty of warning that a train was approaching. *Mike Jose*

A 'Western' class locomotive as the majority of enthusiasts will remember them – in corporate blue livery with full yellow ends. Here, No.D1006 *Western Stalwart* is seen at Reading heading an up express on 1st April 1967. This machine entered traffic in July 1962 in maroon livery with yellow bufferbeams and gained standard yellow warning panels in December of the same year. A full repaint into blue livery was carried out in early 1967, the locomotive being released into service on 22nd March, so it had only been in traffic a few days when photographed in the gleaming condition seen here. It was withdrawn in April 1975, less than nine months after being repainted blue at Laira. *Roy Denison*

In the early stages of the switch to blue livery locomotives of many classes were painted with small yellow warning panels and seven 'Westerns' were out-shopped in this style; they were Nos. D1017/30/6/7/43/7/57. Here, the last-mentioned locomotive, No.D1057 *Western Chieftain* is seen threading Sydney Gardens at the approach to Bath Spa station on 4th October 1968 with a train destined for Bristol. This short stretch of line through the neatly manicured gardens is one of the highlights of the London to Bristol run. In addition there are very ornate bridges, as seen here, but passengers aboard passing trains would have to be very quick-sighted to spot them. *Western Chieftain* ran in this livery until late 1971 when it underwent an overhaul and emerged in early 1972 in blue with full yellow ends. *Colin Caddy*

BR/MAYBACH TYPE 4 C-C 'WESTERN' (CLASS 52)

A familiar and unmistakable backdrop. The 12.30pm Paddington to Plymouth train, headed by an unidentified 'Western', awaits departure from Exeter St David's on 1st May 1969. Note the locomotive is in maroon livery with full yellow ends, which was applied to more than a dozen locomotives in the fleet. There have been three stations on this site, the first dating from 1844; when this was demolished another station was built by the Bristol & Exeter Railway. The structure seen here was constructed by the GWR between 1910 and 1912. *David Wigley*

BR/MAYBACH TYPE 4 C-C 'WESTERN' (CLASS 52)

An unidentified up train has just breasted Dainton summit and heads for its next station stop, probably at Newton Abbot. The train's engine is 'Western' C-C No.D1030 *Western Musketeer*, one of a small number of these locomotives out-shopped from Swindon works in the early days of blue livery with a small yellow warning panel. It was the first 'Western' to be repainted blue, the shade being experimental chromatic blue, not rail blue; the small BR emblem was apparently hand painted. No.D1030 ran in this condition from August 1966 until April 1970 when it was repainted into corporate blue livery with full yellow ends. *Colour Rail.com*

BR/MAYBACH TYPE 4 C-C 'WESTERN' (CLASS 52)

A blot on the landscape? The 8.55am Tavistock Junction to Severn Tunnel Junction freight runs alongside Marine Parade at Dawlish on a June day in 1970. Obviously, the two ladies in conversation on the promenade, who are apparently oblivious to the passing train, are not 'Western' enthusiasts! The locomotive is in absolutely deplorable external condition and clearly well overdue for a repaint, its supposedly yellow warning panel being so dirty and faded one is bound to question its effectiveness as a safety device. The bodyside that is visible also seems to be extremely dirty with little maroon paint showing through the grime. The eastern portal of the 209 yards-long Kennaway tunnel can be seen in the background; this is one of five tunnels between Dawlish and Teignmouth. *Mike Jose*

BR/MAYBACH TYPE 4 C-C 'WESTERN' (CLASS 52)

A picture taken at Truro on 7th September 1971 showing the 8.30am from Paddington to Penzance departing behind 'Western' No.D1056 *Western Sultan*. Note that at this date the carriage formations on the London to West-of-England services still included Mk.1 vehicles in addition to early Mk.2 coaches. No.D1056 entered traffic from Crewe works in early March 1963 and was initially painted maroon with small yellow panels. In September 1967 it was repainted once again in maroon but this time with full yellow ends, and these colours lasted until April 1971 when it emerged from overhaul in the blue livery seen here. Three years later it received further body attention at Laira and survived to become one of the last active 'Westerns', being eventually taken out of service in December 1976. Note the slightly off-centre square ventilator on the front cab sheeting. The 'Westerns' driving cabs, which had large glass windscreens but no external doors, could become extremely hot in the summer and five members of the class (Nos.D1012/28/39/56/71) were fitted with this device in an attempt to increase ventilation – note the driver's sliding window is open. Regrettably, however, this modification provided little improvement and the locomotive crews continued to suffer! *Nick Tindall*

BR/MAYBACH TYPE 4 C-C 'WESTERN' (CLASS 52)

A BR member of staff, perhaps the train's guard, looks on as 'Western' C-C No.D1005 *Western Venturer* is attached to a Sheffield train at Penzance on 22nd July 1975. The locomotive appears to be displaying an incorrect train reporting number; perhaps the crew had not yet altered the number in the headcode box. One wonders how many photographers have taken a shot of a 'Western' at this precise spot despite the inconveniently sited platform lamp standard – perhaps it could be called the 'standard' Penzance shot? No.D1005 was one of the longest serving 'Westerns', having entered traffic in June 1962, and it would probably have survived into 1977 had it not been for a small fire in November 1976 which prompted its immediate withdrawal from service. *Roy Denison*

Yes, it's *Western Venturer* once again! Photographed in soft evening light on 13th August 1976, No.D1005 descends the 1 in 66 gradient at the bottom of Rattery bank and approaches Totnes with an up van train, probably newspaper empties destined for Paddington. The relatively unusual first and third vehicles are later-build 'Syphon G' vans, originally a GWR design. They came to be used as general purpose parcels vans, the last being constructed by BR as late as 1955. The coach is a brake second corridor (BSK) which was doubtless included in the formation to provide basic passenger accommodation for home-going shift workers on very early morning trains from Paddington. In addition to the GWR-designed vans and the Mk.1 BSK, Southern Railway-designed vans are also included in the formation – what an assortment! *Chris Evans*

An unmistakable location. An up freight, hauled by 'Western' Class No.D1030 *Western Musketeer,* has just passed through Dawlish station and heads towards Exeter on 24th March 1976. Note that the train's consist includes sheeted china clay wagons, probably *en route* to Stoke-on-Trent. No.D1030 was originally scheduled to be built at Swindon but (as previously mentioned) construction of Nos.D1030 to D1034 was transferred to Crewe to relieve pressure on the former works. This machine was officially withdrawn in April 1976 so its days were very much numbered when this shot was taken. This locomotive was the first 'Western' to receive blue livery, the shade being experimental chromatic blue (see page 88).
Hugh Ballantyne

BR/MAYBACH TYPE 4 C-C 'WESTERN' (CLASS 52)

The previous shot was clearly taken on a rather gloomy day – the sun did not always deign to shine at Dawlish, especially in March! This picture, taken from about the same spot but looking eastwards, shows entirely different conditions because it was taken during the hot summer of 1976 and depicts a rather travel-stained 'Western' Class No.D1001 *Western Pathfinder* nearing Dawlish station on 14th August with the 9.30am Paddington to Penzance train which is largely made up of non air-conditioned Mk.2 stock. *Western Pathfinder,* as mentioned elsewhere in this book, was withdrawn some weeks later following a collision. *Chris Evans*

Towards the end of the reign of the 'Westerns' on the WR many examples were in traffic after their planned withdrawal date due to the unreliability of other motive power and the external condition of many can only be described as 'absolutely deplorable'. Here, in this picture No.D1015 *Western Champion* is seen 'on the stops' at Paddington on 22nd May 1976 after arrival from the west of England. Quite large areas of the bodyside are totally devoid of paint and also parts of the roof appear to have paint missing. One of the causes of this was over zealous application of acidic cleaning fluid which was sometimes insufficiently washed off. Overhauls at Swindon had come to an end by 1973 and it fell to Laira to maintain the fleet as best it could using components from early withdrawals. In an effort to keep the class looking presentable Laira started a repainting programme and around fifty members of the class were treated in the 1973-76 period. What a come down! *Chris Evans*

Substituting for a 'Blue Pullman' diesel-electric unit that was presumably out of service for repair, a Brush Type 4 Co-Co hauling a 'scratch' rake of Pullman cars accelerates away from its Solihull station stop. No.D1683, in the original two-tone green livery which really suited these locomotives, was in charge of the 4.50pm Paddington to Wolverhampton (Low Level) service on 1st September 1964. This machine entered traffic in October 1963 at Old Oak Common depot and was one of those Brush Type 4s that displaced the 'Westerns' on the London to Birmingham/Wolverhampton line. Note the make-up of the Pullman train which includes really vintage vehicles at the front followed by a trio of much more modern Metro-Cammell cars. One wonders what the regular clientele on this train preferred; it was a choice between the modern but notoriously rough-riding diesel units, the equally modern but somewhat characterless Metro-Cammell carriages or the faded opulence of the pre-war coaches. *Michael Mensing*

Opposite top: In the early 1960s the rapid elimination of steam traction was seen as a top priority and BR was looking for a lightweight Type 4 diesel-electric locomotive capable of producing at least 2,500hp and had been encouraged by the success of No.D0260 *Lion* which employed a Sulzer 12LDA28-C 12 cylinder engine. Brush Traction developed a 2,750hp Co-Co design, known as the Brush Type 4, and a total of 512 machines was eventually constructed, 310 at the Brush works in Loughborough and the remainder by BR at Crewe; the locomotives were built over a 5 year period from September 1962 to January 1968. They weighed around 115 tons but it should be noted that there were significant differences depending on the type of train heating equipment fitted. In the early 1970s it was decided to de-rate the power output of the class to 2,580hp in order to reduce stresses on the power plant and thereby improve reliability. The ubiquitous Brush Type 4s were extremely versatile machines and could be found on a wide variety of workings ranging from express passenger to slow-moving coal trains. Most were originally painted in two-tone green livery and No.D1951 shows off its colours to good effect, being almost brand-new when this portrait was taken on 15th October 1966. It was working the southbound 'Pines Express' from Manchester to Poole and was photographed near The Hawthorns Halt, between Wolverhampton (Low Level) and Birmingham (Snow Hill), at a time when this train was routed via Crewe and Shrewsbury. No.D1951 has had quite an eventful life, becoming No.47 507 in February 1974 under the TOPS re-numbering scheme and it was re-numbered again in March 1985 and this time became No.47 716 after being selected for use on a new, recast, push-pull Glasgow to Aberdeen service. No.47 716 ended its career with Network South-East. *Michael Mensing*

Opposite bottom: An unidentified Brush Type 4 heads southwards at the site of the former Dorrington station, between Shrewsbury and Craven Arms, on 28th March 1970. These machines were, as previously mentioned, equally at home on both passenger and freight workings and in this instance the locomotive is hauling a long coal train. A total of 81 of these locomotives was built without train heating apparatus and confined to freight-only operations during the winter months but they could, of course, be used on passenger trains during the summer. The structure in the foreground is part of the old station which was closed to passengers from 9th June 1958. In the background the distinctive signal box is visible and (what appears to have been) a passing loop into which slow-moving southbound trains could be recessed. *John Spencer Gilks*

BRUSH TYPE 4 Co-Co (CLASS 47)

Tunnel portals do not come much finer than this! Photographed on 26th August 1975, Brush Type 4 No.47 247 emerges from the western end of Box tunnel, between Chippenham and Bath, with a down empty coal train. The tunnel takes its name from a village located at its western end. There used to be a station at Box but this was closed from 4th January 1965. No.47 247 entered service in January 1966 as No.D1924 at Cardiff (Canton) shed. This locomotive was originally equipped with a steam heating boiler but this would have been removed sometime during the 1970s/80s as steam heated stock was slowly phased out; the locomotive would then have had no heating capability. *Hugh Ballantyne*

Opposite top: The south end of Hereford station is the location of this shot that apparently shows a civil engineer's ballast train 'waiting the road'. This picture was taken on 24th November 1971 and the locomotive in view is No.1721. This engine was built by Brush and entered service in March 1964 at Cardiff (Canton) shed; it was later re-numbered 47 130, withdrawn in March 1988 and cut-up by MC Metal Processors of Glasgow in November 1990. *Colour Rail.com*

Opposite bottom: Versatility personified. Previous illustrations in this section depict Brush Type 4s on passenger duty, hauling a coal train and powering a civil engineer's ballast working and here is one on a parcels train! The location is unmistakable: yes, it is Penzance, and this shot shows No.47 032 pulling out of the station on 9th September 1975 with a long parcels train bound for somewhere on the London Midland Region. At this time BR still conveyed a lot of newspaper and general parcels traffic and a network of trains like this one, made up of an amazing jumble of vans of widely differing origins, shapes and sizes, were a familiar sight throughout the system. In the early 1980s the newspaper printing industry switched to road transport and today's courier companies have grabbed the remaining traffic with the result that these trains, which added an extra dimension to the railway scene, are no longer seen. No.47 032 was originally No.D1611, a Crewe product, which entered service in August 1964. *Chris Evans*

A scene at Magor, between Newport and Severn Tunnel Junction, showing Brush Type 4 No.47 513 whisking a freight eastwards on a sunny 30th July 1977. There used to be a station serving Magor but it was closed from 2nd November 1964. When this photograph was taken No.47 513 had been in service ten years, being introduced as D1959 in February 1967 following completion by Brush Traction Ltd In May 1979 it was named *Severn*. *Hugh Ballantyne*

Opposite: Autumn tints abound on the lineside trees as an unidentified Brush Type 4 in sparkling ex-works condition heads westwards from Reading in charge of the 10.55am Paddington to Paignton train on 27th October 1977. The rectangular plate under the driver's window indicates that this machine was a Crewe-built locomotive. The 'Westerns' had gone by the time of this photograph and the best that could hoped for on a loco-hauled WR express to and from London was a Brush Type 4 or an English Electric Type 4 (Class 50). The light engine on the up line is Brush Type 2 No.31 307. *Nick Tindall*

BRUSH TYPE 4 Co-Co (CLASS 47) ————————————

An international skyline? Some of the modern skyscrapers of Birmingham's city centre form the backdrop to this picture of Brush Type 4 No.47 468 negotiating a very tight curve at Bordesley Junction with a Birmingham to London Paddington via Oxford train on 24th February 1979. Prior to the closure of Snow Hill station trains from Birmingham to Paddington would have had a direct run along the tracks that are just visible in the foreground on the extreme left of the picture. The concentration of all Birmingham main line services on New Street station in the late 1960s meant that some trains on the former WR routes had to use devious and circuitous routes as seen here. The photographer states that this train actually started out as the 9.55am Paddington to Worcester (Shrub Hill) which obviously continued to Birmingham on an interesting circular diagram. Regrettably, the diagram does not appear to have included a trip through a washing machine at any stage: note the dreadful condition of the leading coaches. *Michael Mensing*

BRUSH TYPE 4 Co-Co (CLASS 47)

An absolutely stunning photograph of an unidentified Brush Type 4 approaching Goring & Streatley on 12th December 1981 just after a heavy snowfall. Note how the powdery snow is being whipped up by the momentum of the train. *Roy Denison*

The later 'Inter-City' units built for the Western Region were, perhaps, the most stylish and best appointed first generation diesel multiple units produced by BR. In this picture an eight-car formation is seen descending the Lickey incline, presumably with a train bound for Cardiff, in 1964. The units were based on the Mk. 1 coach design, fitted with four 230hp Albion engines and mounted on B4 bogies which gave a very smooth ride. Note the very distinctive gangwayed front end with its bright yellow gangway shield and wrap-around windows. The latter were a really attractive design feature but later proved a maintenance headache due to the ingress of rainwater. Note also the very commodious brake van which occupies almost a third of the vehicle's length. These units had a high degree of insulation from noise and draughts and were equipped with particularly comfortable seating throughout. Ten four-car units were constructed, five of which incorporated a buffet car. Initially, the units were based at Cardiff and employed principally on services to Derby plus one or two turns to Plymouth. The coach nearest to the camera in this photograph is No.W52091, a second class driving motor coach with a brake van and lavatory accommodation which was officially known as a DMBSL type vehicle; it had 32 seats in a saloon. This carriage entered traffic in May 1963 and was withdrawn in August 1984, its operational life no doubt being cut short due to the fact that it was insulated with blue asbestos that was very expensive to remove and, no doubt, withdrawal was seen as an easier option when a second generation of diesel units was starting to come on stream. *Michael Mensing*

In 1965 the 'Inter-City' units were transferred to the Cardiff-Bristol-Portsmouth service, but their tenure on this route was short-lived and they were soon moved to Reading depot for use on the Paddington to Oxford service. In 1970 the buffet cars were removed from the units, thus reducing five units to three cars only. Surprisingly, one of the redundant buffet cars found a new lease of life as an electric multiple unit vehicle in a Class 309. In this photograph the 7.35am from Oxford is depicted entering Paddington station on 7th May 1974 with unit No.L712 leading (what appears to be) a ten-car formation with two vehicles being hidden from view on the straight section between the crossovers. The coach at the front of the train is the same type as the vehicle nearest to the camera in the previous picture, but its appearance has been radically altered. In addition to blue/grey livery the carriage now sports an all-over yellow front end in place of a yellow shield which has been superseded by a standard gangway shield. *Chris Evans*

SWINDON-BUILT 'INTER-CITY' UNITS (CLASS 123)

The elevated motorway flyover in the background immediately identifies the location of this picture – the approach to London's Paddington station. Here, three-car unit No.L715 leads the 4.02pm Paddington to Reading past Royal Oak on 29th July 1975; on the rear is four-car unit No.L712. The front coach is W52096 a 56-seat compartment vehicle which consisted of four no smoking and three smoking compartments separated by a vestibule; there were two toilets at the far end of the coach. After working on the Oxford route for some time all of the units were later moved northwards to Hull for use on services to Sheffield and Manchester, where they ended their days in 1984. These units were arguably the best in terms of passenger comfort produced under the modernisation plan and it is to be regretted that no examples were preserved. *Chris Evans*

A close-up portrait of vehicle No.W52095, included principally for the benefit of modellers, showing the B4 bogies with which these units were fitted and the arrangement of the engines and fuel tanks. Note that the grey-painted area varied on these units, some included the door adjacent to the cab, as seen here, but others did not and looked rather strange as a result. This shot was taken at Bristol Temple Meads station in May 1976. Note the somewhat anachronistic tail lamp – presumably the unit had red blinds fitted in the route indicator boxes. On the Southern Region signalmen were instructed to accept a red blind as indicating the rear of a train but WR signalmen were not, so a tail lamp had to be displayed in the traditional way. *Colour Rail.com*

SWINDON-BUILT 'INTER-CITY' UNITS (CLASS 123)

The WR's policy to 'go it alone' with locomotives using hydraulic transmission was always controversial but, perhaps, the strangest decision of all was that to order a fleet of moderately powered diesel locomotives for yard and trip working just at a time when this kind of work was starting to decline. It was almost as if some BR departments were totally oblivious to what was happening in the 'real' railway world outside! Twenty-six 48½-ton, 650hp machines were ordered from Swindon works in June 1963 and a further order was subsequently placed for thirty locomotives. The locomotives were equipped with a Paxman Ventura 6YJXL engine and had Voith transmission, and the first one came off the production line in July 1964. Some examples lasted only three or four years with BR and found further use in heavy industry but, even here, the decline in the mining and steel industries led to many being declared redundant well before their time and snapped up by the preservation movement. Other locomotives were actually sold for scrap by BR when barely four years old, thus adding to the misery of the British taxpayer! No.D9555 proved to be the very last locomotive built at Swindon for use in Great Britain (some locomotives were built in 1979 for use in Kenya) so the works hardly went out on a high note after an otherwise very illustrious history. The locomotive seen here posing outside Swindon works on 27th September 1964 is No.D9513, a locomotive that was withdrawn by BR after less than 3½ years' work. Even so, it survived into preservation and at the time of writing can be observed on the Embsay & Bolton Abbey Railway in Yorkshire. *Colin Caddy*

SWINDON-BUILT TYPE 1 0-6-0 (CLASS 14)

No.D9500 – the doyen of a class that should never have been built. At least this shot provides conclusive proof that these locomotives did some work for BR before they were sold off for industrial use. This picture was taken at Cardiff (Canton) in March 1968 and, incredibly, No.D9500, the oldest locomotive in the fleet which entered service in July 1964, was among the last batch to be taken out of traffic in April 1969. No.D9500 subsequently survived into preservation while other examples were exported to Spain where, presumably, they were re-gauged for further use. One wonders if they still exist! *Colour Rail.com*

ENGLISH ELECTRIC TYPE 4 Co-Co (CLASS 50)

The up 'Golden Hind', the 4.57am from Penzance to Paddington, with No.50 014 *Warspite* in charge, has just passed the site of Burlescombe station and approaches Whiteball tunnel on 19th May 1979. The train is climbing on a 1 in 115 gradient at this point but such an incline is unlikely to have troubled such a powerful locomotive pulling a modest 9-coach formation. No.50 014 entered traffic in May 1968 and was allocated to the LMWL (London Midland Western Lines) for use on Anglo-Scottish trains north of Crewe; it was named in May 1978. Unfortunately, nine years later *Warspite* became one of the very first members of this class to be withdrawn from service, an event that occurred in December 1987, and it was cut-up at Vic Berry's, Leicester, yard in May 1989. *Hugh Ballantyne*

Opposite top: In 1962 English Electric constructed a 2,700hp Type 4 Co-Co locomotive and BR provided facilities for 'road tests' which was a fancy name for using the machine in everyday traffic for evaluation purposes. This locomotive, No.DP2, which weighed 105 tons, had a 16 cylinder 16CSVT engine and developed a maximum tractive effort of 55,000lb. It had the appealing appearance of a 'Deltic', but was destined to have a short working life, being damaged beyond repair in a collision at Thirsk in 1967. BR must have been impressed by the design because they ordered 50 examples, Nos.D400-D449, which were initially hired from the manufacturer; they were purchased outright in about 1973. The class, which like their older sisters was known at that time as English Electric Type 4, was earmarked for use on the West Coast Main Line (WCML) between Crewe and Scotland and, usually, trains powered by this class were double-headed to cope with the fierce gradients on that route. The locomotives (designated Class 50 under TOPS) were unreliable, however, and this led to a standing joke among crews that passengers only had a 50:50 chance of reaching their destination on time. In 1974, when the northern section of the WCML was electrified, the entire fleet was moved to the WR primarily for use on services from London to Bristol, Oxford and the West Country. In the late 1970s it was decided to name the locomotives after Royal Navy warships, No.50 035 *Ark Royal* being the first beneficiary of this policy. In 1979 a refurbishment programme was started at Doncaster which involved simplifying the complex electronics in order to improve reliability and removing redundant equipment such as slow speed control. The air intake fan arrangement, which apparently functioned well overseas but was affected by the damp British climate, was also modified. Following refurbishment the class was allocated to two depots, Laira and Old Oak Common, but the class's reliability problems were never fully overcome and the first member was withdrawn in early 1987; the last examples were withdrawn in 1994. In this picture No.50 045 passes Totnes on the up through line and prepares for the assault on Dainton bank with the 11.00am Plymouth to Paddington train on 13th August 1976. The locomotive was unnamed at this time but was christened in April 1978, becoming *Achilles*. No.50 045 was withdrawn in December 1990. *Chris Evans*

Opposite bottom: The summer of 1976 will be long remembered as one of the hottest in living memory and many people in this photograph are clearly taking advantage of the Mediterranean conditions to take a dip in the sea, apparently oblivious to No.50 030 passing by only a few yards away. Some folk always get their priorities wrong! This picture shows the Kensington (Olympia) to St Austell 'Motorail' train heading west at the approach to Dawlish station on 14th August 1976. BR introduced car carrying trains way back in the mid-1950s and in 1966 coined the brand name 'Motorail' for what had developed into a quite impressive network of services which included overnight trains with sleeping accommodation in addition to the daytime services. Trains operated from London to many destinations in Scotland while on the WR places served included Plymouth, Penzance and Fishguard, from where boat connections ran to Ireland. No.50 030 was built by English Electric as No.D430 and entered service in July 1968; it was re-numbered in March 1974 and named *Repulse* in April 1978. *Chris Evans*

ENGLISH ELECTRIC TYPE 4 Co-Co (CLASS 50)

In 1980 No.50 023 *Howe* became the first example to be painted in a revised, eye-catching livery consisting of wrap around yellow-painted cabs, large bodyside numerals and BR logo; this colourful livery became known as 'BR Blue Large Logo'. Other liveries were also used in later years, but these are outside the remit of this book. Here, Nos.50 003 *Temeraire* and 50 002 *Superb*, both of which sport the new style livery, provide super power for the 6.40am Totnes to Exeter St David's train which is seen leaving Newton Abbot – presumably such a powerful combination made a very brisk getaway! This working presumably started from Plymouth Laira and was no doubt a convenient way of moving locomotives and rolling stock from there to Exeter. The photographer adds that there was an evening balancing working which was advertised to terminate at Totnes, the empty stock presumably proceeding directly to Laira. Did somebody say the railway ran for the benefit of the passengers? *Terry Phillips*

ENGLISH ELECTRIC TYPE 4 Co-Co (CLASS 50)

For years BR was ridiculed by a large number of detractors, but even the fiercest critic would have to concede that, apart from running the national system on a shoestring, the High Speed Train (HST) was one of its greatest achievements. Many people would probably justifiably say that the HST was a world-beater because it is the world's fastest diesel train. The prototype HST first appeared in 1972 and consisted of two power cars, one at each end of a rake of ten Mk.3 passenger coaches. The 2,250hp, 68.5 tonnes power cars had 12RP200L Paxman Valenta engines which powered frame-mounted Brush traction motors and the permitted top speed of an HST was 125mph, so this train undoubtedly revolutionised Inter-city travel in Great Britain. Initially, the HST was considered to be two locomotives formed at either end of a rake of coaches, and the power cars were designated Class 41 and numbered 41001 and 41002. The formation consisted of four trailer second and four trailer first coaches, a kitchen car and a buffet car. Shortly after the train's introduction BR had a rethink and decided to classify the entire formation as a diesel electric multiple unit and it was renumbered into a new number series for HST and ATP vehicles, the power vehicles becoming Nos.43000 and 43001. Two trailer carriages were transferred for use in the royal train which was being enhanced in connection with HM the Queen's Silver Jubilee celebrations. One of the power cars was scrapped in December 1990 but the other car, No.41001, is preserved as part of the National Collection and, at the time of writing, is undergoing restoration to working order; other vehicles survive in everyday service. The prototype set entered revenue-earning service on the Western Region and in this picture is seen nearing journey's end at Royal Oak forming the 1.48pm Weston-super-Mare to Paddington train on 29th July 1975, this working being part of its regular diagram at this time; it later worked the 4.45pm service to Bristol Temple Meads. *Chris Evans*

PROTOTYPE HIGH SPEED TRAIN

The HST takeover at Paddington. The first fleet of HSTs was known as Class 253 and they entered service on the WR in 1976, operating between London and Weston-super-Mare, and Swansea. In this portrait, taken on the evening of 7th March 1978, unit Nos.253 023 and 253 008 are seen waiting in platforms 4 and 5 respectively while in Platform 6 is another unidentified HST with power car No.W43051 erupting into life nearest to the buffer stops which are out of sight on the left. The HSTs employed on the WR were seven car units whereas those introduced on the Eastern Region two years later consisted of eight coaches and were known as Class 254. Paddington has one of the most elegant train sheds in Great Britain to which this picture bears ample testament. *Chris Evans*

HIGH SPEED TRAINS

The maximum service speed of High Speed Trains, as previously mentioned, was 125mph but it is unlikely that the HST seen here passing through Goring & Streatley on 12th December 1981 was travelling at anything approaching that speed given the arctic conditions and the fact that the train was on the local line; perhaps the fast line was temporarily out of use due to frozen points. The front end of the leading power car is encrusted with snow thus making identification of the unit impossible, however the rare combination of sunshine and deep snow have produced a splendid shot, so does it really matter? The photographer is to be congratulated on venturing out on such a bitterly cold day, but perhaps he lived locally ... *Roy Denison*

Overleaf: A Bristol 'cityscape'. The HST units were designed to compete with coach services plus the domestic airlines and on the London to Bristol route a substantial threat was posed to BR's passenger business by the M4 motorway. Photographed against a background of city skyscrapers, unit No.253 018 passes Bristol East depot bound for Paddington on 2nd May 1979. At that time BR's freight business was undergoing major upheavals and traditional short wheelbase goods wagons and their accompanying guard's brake vans were being rapidly phased out, but the yards depicted here were reasonably full of such vehicles – perhaps they were merely stored out of use awaiting disposal. *Hugh Ballantyne*